5 Five Minutes More

by Sybil Jason

BearManor Media
2007

Five Minutes More
© 2007 Sybil Jason
All rights reserved.

"An Interviewer's Dream"
© 2007 Leonard Maltin

For information. address:

BearManor Media
P. O. Box 71426
Albany, GA 31708

bearmanormedia.com

Cover design by John Teehan

Typesetting and layout by John Teehan

Published in the USA by BearManor Media

ISBN—1-59393-115-8

I dedicate both my books, My Fifteen Minutes *and* Five Minutes More *to my dear sister Anita. If not but for her love, guidance, and dedication, my career would not have existed and neither would the stories I have written about within their pages.*

To my beloved husband, Anthony Drake who stood behind me in everything that I did I owe him my love and my gratitude into eternity.

The International Sybil Jason Fan Club
President: Gary L. Heckman
745 S. 31st
Lincoln, Nebraska   68510
USA
Email: glheckman@juno.com

Table of Contents

Acknowledgements i

An Interviewer's Dream iii
   by Leonard Maltin

Five Minutes More v
   by Sybil Jason

The Child Star Syndrome 1

The Second Time Around 3

A Potpourri of Talent 9

When Silence Was Truly Golden 65

Vaudevillians Supreme 81

Dem Guys 85

Second Banana Scene Stealers 91

Us "Kids" 97

Expiration Date 125

Index 129

Acknowledgements

First and foremost, I must thank my son-in-law, Phillip Rossi, for continually getting me out of computer pickles while writing this book. I admit that the many and vast advantages that computers afford the writer are quite beyond my ken, so I had the advantage of Phil's expertise.

I thank my beloved daughter, Toni Maryanna Rossi, for standing solidly behind me with encouragement and offers of help in many and varied ways. Thanks to her expertise with the camera, I was able to put in a new picture of myself at the back of this book and several snapshots that she has taken at various times.

Although my beloved husband, Anthony Drake, passed away in 2005 I still feel his encouragement daily. He was behind me all of the way when I was writing *My Fifteen Minutes* and was extremely proud when it was published. I think he would have liked *Five Minutes More*.

I thank Ned Comstock of the University of Southern California, for his ongoing help and answers to my endless questions of research.

I also thank multi talented singer-actor Richard Halpern for all the help he has offered me throughout the years.

To the president of my international fan club, Gary Heckman, who convinced me that a Sybil Jason fan club was necessary even though I didn't think we'd last a year - but are now in our 23rd year of existence.

Let me count the ways that the vice president of my fan club, Ruth Pollack, has assisted me with a cheerful smile on her face.

To the whole Berkowitz family, especially Saville, for enriching my collection of childhood photos, some of which I have never seen before.

To producer-writer Chet Dowling, who I never had to ask for help because it was always given so freely and generously without the asking, 24-7.

To Stan and Val Ball of England, with Val's inspiring contribution of a 23,000-cross-stitch reproduction of a photo of Al Jolson and me.

To Brother Alan ZoDDA for his ever inspiring religious strength and friendship.

To Pastor Bob Bock, who got me through the most vulnerable time in my life when my beloved husband passed away.

To Hollywood historian Leonard Maltin for reading my first book…and enjoying it!

To Dave Greim, for his generosity of spirit and helping hand.

To George Hudson of Canada, for his ongoing interest and help.

To Professor Paul Bowers of New York University for his generosity in supplying photographs.

To fellow authors Richard Grudens and Brian Decker for applauding my writing efforts.

To Bob King, editor and general manager of the excellent magazine, *Classic Images*.

To *Classic Images*' top notch reviewer and fellow authoress, Laura Wagner, for reviewing and enjoying my book and saying so!

To all the gang at Warner Bros., led by Leith Adams, for their ongoing help.

And to the best publisher in the world…Ben Ohmart, who puts his heart and soul into everything that he does.

And finally…much love and respect go to my favorite contemporaries who have been my cheering committee and treasured friends…Delmar and Antoinette Watson, Ann Rutherford, Joan Leslie, Bobby Mauch, and Dick and Betty Jones.

An Interviewer's Dream
by Leonard Maltin

When I started interviewing movie people many years ago, I learned that most of them fell into one of two categories: those who paid attention to what was going on around them and had interesting stories to tell, and those who didn't. Some of the latter group were perfectly pleasant; they just didn't have much to say.

Every rare now and then I'd encounter a film veteran who was an interviewer's dream: someone who was observant, didn't make him or herself the centerpiece of every story, and had a gift for framing incidents as anecdotes.

Sybil Jason is just such a person. She proved it in her charming book *My Fifteen Minutes*. Even that title tells you that she has a sense of perspective about her screen career…and a sense of humor, too.

I'm so glad Sybil has decided to tap her reservoir of memory once more. As an old-movie nut, I lap up stories about the period so many of us consider the Golden Age of Hollywood. There aren't many people left who can offer first-hand stories we haven't all heard before. Sybil Jason can. She drops names like Guy Kibbee, Kay Francis, and Glenda Farrell, and fills in details about these wonderful personalities that help us appreciate what they were like off-camera. What's more, she recounts her experiences with warmth and enthusiasm.

If you love that Golden Age, you're bound to enjoy this book. Sit back and let Sybil Jason take you on a journey to a time and place that may seem exotic to most of us…but was absolutely real to a little girl who loved what she was doing, and still cherishes those memories.

– Leonard Maltin

Five Minutes More
by Sybil Jason

I never in my wildest dreams thought that I would ever be writing a second book. In fact, when the notion first hit me to write my first one, *My Fifteen Minutes*, I wasn't sure that I had enough material to turn even that into a book. Much to my amazement once I got started the memories just flooded in like water gushing from a tap.

I started with my birth in Cape Town, South Africa, a bit of family history, my start on the stage at the age of three and what led me ultimately to London and then finally to America with a movie contract in my hands to become Warner Bros.' first child star under a long-term contract.

However, the very meat of the book was that I had dedicated each chapter to some of the greatest icons of the movie industry and my personal experiences with them. I am sure you would have come across at least one or two of your favorite stars as the list included amongst many others, Errol Flynn, Lana Turner, Humphrey Bogart, Shirley Temple, Al Jolson, Judy Garland, even Marilyn Monroe and the man who was my bodyguard for a short time, the real Eliot Ness.

Most people have asked me why my successful career came to such an abrupt end and I have explained all of that in *My Fifteen Minutes,* so it would be redundant to repeat it here. However, much to the delight of this author, readers of my first book have been writing letters asking when they could expect another book from me as they very much enjoyed my first one. I mulled that over for quite a while and decided there were a lot of memories still left. I tested a list of names on my publisher and some book reviewers of the stars that I next intended to write about. I received their enthusiastic endorsement mainly because so little had been written about these people due to the fact that history had categorized them in a secondary place in the Hollywood Sun. Apart from anything else that was my deciding factor to write another book. I always had a twinge of guilt leaving out so many wonderful people in my first book, but as a neophyte author I was advised, while trying to get a publisher, to entice them with the biggest names that I could legitimately use in my personal experiences.

In my eyes, no matter what their category, they all exhibited that magical quality that was hard to define. It was never anything so obvious like coming on like gangbusters. On the contrary, for the most part, they were quite retiring in their offstage persona, yet one could still feel that magic from just having been in the same room as they were. Secondary? I think not.

The best example I could possibly give you is the contribution that Claude Rains, Sydney Greenstreet, Peter Lorre and Conrad Veidt, amongst others, lent to the movie *Casablanca*. I liken these gentlemen to a good solid cake and the stars of the movie, Humphrey Bogart, Ingrid Bergman and Paul Henreid as the frosting on top of it. Without those combined ingredients the product would be incomplete and uninteresting. Strangely enough, in his later years, Bogie, who played my father in the movie *The Great O'Malley*, became the cake with his outstanding performances in *The Treasure of Sierra Madre* and *The African Queen*. No doubt he received some fine assistance at various times from Walter Huston and Katharine Hepburn, who were big slabs of solid foundation themselves, but in all of these cases frosting would have been superfluous!

As I mentioned previously, Hollywood deemed who was considered an icon and who were the featured players, but I think I am going to leave that up to the reader to judge. For my part, whether icon or featured, I was fortunate to have benefited by being able to work with the best of them and I wouldn't have traded one pure unadulterated second of it for anything in the world.

The Child Star Syndrome

As long as I can remember I have been a devotee of autobiographies written by people who had long and distinguished careers. However, the career of a child star is notoriously short for a valid reason. Mother Nature rules supreme and because of that very few child stars can lay claim to the successful transition from child to adult.

The very cuteness and precocity that endeared them to the movie-going public was suddenly rejected by their loyal followers once they had outgrown their babyhood and the result of that rejection showed up as lackluster attendance at the box office for their movies.

Naturally, when that happened, the powers-that-be no longer wished to put up their money or time to advance the careers of their former mini-powerhouses and either looked for replacements or concentrated on youngsters in their teens that had already passed the awkward stage.

To be brutally frank, the child stars that *were* given the opportunity to prove themselves as adults did a disservice not only to themselves but to their contemporaries by displaying their cutesy mannerisms and facial expressions of babyhood inappropriately into their new phase of life. That only translated into bad acting and forever left a stigma tied to ex child stars.

Unfortunately for the few youngsters who had the capacity to make the difficult transition, they could not override the bad examples set for them which left a bad taste in the mouths of the producers and casting directors. Those in charge were convinced that all ex-child stars were wrapped up in the same ball of stunted maturity but unfortunately that assumption led to lost opportunities for some amazing talents.

2 Five Minutes More

A Hawaiian pose that was banned for publicity!

However, a few decades later there were wonderful exceptions to the rule like Jodie Foster, Drew Barrymore, Diane Lane, my late friend Roddy McDowall and Ron Howard, whose talents grew alongside of their physical growth. Lucky for all of us, their careers are ongoing to this day.

The Second Time Around

When World War II had ended and I returned to America I still had visions of returning to acting. After all, that is all I had known since I was a baby of two years old.

I almost immediately went into a musical stage production portraying a little Kansas girl that my dear friend Judy Garland had made so very famous. It wasn't quite what I had had in mind but I looked very young for my age and was only a year older than Judy had been when she did *The Wizard of Oz* for MGM, so I figured that it was a start.

The play and I got very good reviews, which encouraged me to get an agent and see if I could start realizing my dream of the ultimate goal of becoming, in time, a good character actress.

There is no doubt that I had enjoyed my career as a child in musicals in some of my movies, but it was in my dramatic roles that I felt most confident and happy. By the time I was almost eleven years old I got closer to my dream by portraying the little cockney slavery girl, Becky, in my friend Shirley Temple's 1939 movie, *The Little Princess*.

In 1947, when I had finished my run in *The Wizard of Oz* and was approaching my eighteenth birthday, I didn't know exactly what was in store for me career-wise but, nevertheless, I headed for Warner Bros. like a homing pigeon.

I must say I was treated beautifully by everyone on the Lot from the highest CEO to the "people behind the scenes" and they all acted like the proud parents of a child who was now approaching adulthood and whom they still afforded their affection and utmost respect.

By this time I had already met my future husband, Tony Drake. One day I had taken him to Warners to introduce him to some of my very favorite people and, as he had a wonderful outgoing personality, everyone took to him…with the exception of one person. I didn't find that out until I returned to the studio a few days later.

REALITY BITES

I must first preface this story by saying that when I first came back to America after the war, I had a bit of immigration trouble due to a mistake that the American Consul had made in South Africa. Instead of coming directly to Hollywood I had to go to Canada and re-apply for a visa to enter the United States. Immigration laws were extremely strict after the war and I ended up staying in Canada for three months with no visa in

This is like getting the cover of *Life* magazine in South Africa.

sight. This was incongruous to me seeing that in 1937, on the eve of the coronation in England, I was named Honorary Princess of Canada and President Roosevelt had named me honorary Secretary of State in this country.

After patiently waiting for three months and nothing new was happening in regards to my return to America, it occurred to me to get in touch with some people in Hollywood who might vouch that I would eventually be employed and who they would stand behind till I was given a permanent visa. I decided to take a chance and I phoned Louella Parsons, Hollywood's top columnist, and Mr. Jack Warner. Bless them both, they got busy and within 48 hours I received my temporary visa, which would eventually be extended into a permanent one once I got reestablished in Hollywood.

That day, when I made a return visit to Warner Bros., I happened to get invited to the office of one of my directors that I had when I was a small girl. He was very affable and happy to see me and it was quite unusual for a director of his prominence to have extended a generous amount of time for my visit.

We reminisced about the old days and then he asked me what my plans were for my future. In my earlier visit to the Lot this gentleman had met Tony, my husband-to-be, and had been most charming to him, but this time he remarked that he thought I would be making a big mistake to become involved with a young man who, as far as he could see, had nothing going for him but his youth! Of *course* Tony was not a mogul or a successful business man. He had just served his country in war time in the Navy for four years and was newly arrived in California from his home state of Pennsylvania and had not yet started on any career. I adored him and was very hurt by my director's opinion of him, but let it go for the time being and we returned to the subject of my career and what hopes I had for it.

My director thought that I had great potential for eventually acquiring stardom again and suggested that he give me a small but important part in his forthcoming production. He felt it would be a good opportunity for me to "get my feet wet" and back into the swing of things. He also informed me that he would like to put me under personal contract to him so that he could guide my career like Mervyn LeRoy had done for my friend Lana Turner. He said in the next few days he would have the contract drawn up and when it was ready I was to return and we could go over it to my satisfaction. In the meantime, the part in his movie was mine. I was very excited and asked if I could give the news to the press because to say the least it would also help me with the immigration people. He assured me that I could go ahead with the announcement.

Tony and I really celebrated that night and we just knew that our future was going to be wonderful and that my permanent residency would soon be a reality.

The next day I called up the famous columnist and my friend since I was a child, Sidney Skolsky, and told him my news. He said that it would make a good story that a director who had guided me as a child star was going to direct me in my first adult part. True to his word it appeared in his column a few days later.

The next week I got a call from my director's secretary telling me that the contract had been drawn up and if it was possible, for me to come in and sign it. Possible? I almost broke all speed records getting there.

When I read it, I couldn't believe how generous it was and I was ready to sign then and there, but my director told me to be a bit more cautious and have my lawyer look it over for approval. I was ecstatic with everything I read in the contract, but was just a little let down that I wasn't asked to sign it right then and there. That evening Tony and my friends convinced me that it was all in my best interests and the next day I was able to see a lawyer recommended to me by one of my friends and all he could say after perusing the whole contract that I was a very lucky girl because everything looked good and certainly pointed to my advantage.

By the time we were through it was too late to phone Warners but the very next morning I phoned my director's office and told his secretary I was ready to come in and sign the contract. Most apologetically she informed me that her boss would be in production and story conferences for most of that whole week, but he had left a message to tell me to go ahead and report to the wardrobe department to get fitted for the clothes I was to wear in the movie. She said the moment he was free she would call me to come in and finalize my contract.

I thought to myself that going to Wardrobe before I had even seen a script was certainly putting the cart before the horse, but, then again, I had been away from Hollywood for six years and the way things were done may have changed a bit in the interim.

It was like old home week when I got up to Wardrobe. All of the women gave me a huge welcome and even Orry-Kelly came out of his office to see what all the noise was about. When he found out that I was there for a fitting he too gave me a welcoming hug.

However, he had a good laugh at my concern of being so short. With amusement he informed me that there were endless tricks they could use like wardrobe and camera angles and could have me looking six feet tall in no time.

Already everyone at Warners was making me feel six feet tall and I prayed that I would do them justice in the confidence that they had in me.

I used all the will power that I possessed in the next two weeks not to call my director's office and likened my anxious state to that of a nervous race horse chomping at the bit at the gate barrier. I couldn't wait to get that script into my hands and then go before the cameras once again.

As most actors and actresses do, one day I was looking through the trade papers and turned to the production schedule listed for Warner Bros. and to my horror I noticed that the movie I was to be in was listed to begin shooting in just three days time.

My hands shook as I dialed my director's office, but much to my relief his secretary put him on the line.

He apologized that he had not gotten in touch with me sooner but explained that I must understand that seeing I was not starring in this movie and that my part was comparatively small, he had confidence that an actress of my experience and without a huge amount of preparation would have no trouble doing the part when it was scheduled to be shot at a later date.

I didn't want to push the subject too hard because he had been nice enough to have written a letter to the immigration department informing them that I was going to be in his next production.

It sounded like that our conversation was coming to a conclusion, but much to my relief he told me to come in that afternoon to finalize my contract as he had a rare afternoon free. I was ushered right into his office as soon as I got there and he took out the contract that my lawyer had sanctioned a good one to sign.

The next few minutes were disastrous!!! He advised me of many things that were *not* listed in the contract that he expected me to do and I am sure that I don't have to draw you a picture of what they were. I was close to being physically sick to my stomach trying to comprehend that this was a man I had known since I was five years old and here he was explaining the rules and regulations of the casting couch.

True enough, this casting couch included a luxurious apartment conveniently located near the studio, a brand-new car, a wardrobe of my choice, and living expenses apart from any money that I earned as an actress. Unbelievably, I had the feeling, as he went down the menu of all of these so-called "advantages," that I should be grateful for his generosity. With my heart pounding out of my chest, I looked him straight in the eye and told him that I was unequivocally turning him down. He smiled and told me not to be so hasty with my decision, but to think it over for the next ten days. I told him that it could be ten days or ten years but the answer would still be the same. I also told him that he had put me in an awkward position by telling me that it was all right to have gotten in touch with the press to inform them I would be in his new movie.

He smiled once again and while gently leading me toward the door he said that the part was still mine regardless of the "contract" and that his secretary would let me know when to pick up the script and when to report for the shoot.

I only phoned his office twice after that but on the second call, his secretary, being a very sweet and sensitive lady, told me that, unfortunately, her boss often did this same thing to a lot of young ladies and she advised me that the best thing I could do was just to forget the whole thing. She said that she had the greatest respect for me and wished me all the luck in the world and was sure that with my talent I would be back to making movies in no time. Through this experience I got a clear idea what my contemporaries were going through and I knew I would *never* be willing to lower my morals for *any* reason. I decided then and there that life was too short to face anything like this again.

Funnily enough, after Tony and I were married, we bumped into this man at the famous Brown Derby restaurant and he did greet us, but made sure that Tony knew that he was dining with all of his lawyers at his table that day. Afterwards, Tony and I had a good laugh at that one! I know many of you would have wanted me to name this man but I decided against it because there are still friends and family members of his alive today and I would not like to cause them as much embarrassment as he caused me.

A Potpourri of Talent

Some of the stories you are about to read actually do include some major stars, but for the most part it will be a potpourri of featured players, icons of the music industry and even stars from the silent era.

No matter what their category, icon or otherwise, everyone exhibited a magic that is hard to define. To me I could never really differentiate what it was that placed the talents of the character actors and featured players apart from those who were judged the legitimized stars of the industry.

PETAH PETAH PETAH

Bette Davis never said that, you know, but she will always be remembered by that phrase as long as imitators do a send-up of her while they exaggerate puffing away madly on a cigarette with hand on hip and staring bug eyed out at their amused audiences.

When I was five years old, I wanted to be Bette Davis! I can just hear some of you saying what a lot of hogwash that a child of such a tender age would know enough about the actress to want to grow up to be just like her. Well, folks, when you were under contract to Warner Bros., it didn't matter what age you were, it was mandatory that you attend the preview of every Warners movie whether you were in it or not. Ergo, I think I saw every Bette Davis movie that she made at the studio throughout the thirties.

Because I was Warner Bros.' own child star I was afforded many luxurious perks and not the least of all of them was a full-sized trailer that was always kept on the soundstage that I was working on at the moment.

After consulting with my sister Anita, they found out that my favorite color was blue, so they tailor made the interior in that shade and the trailer itself had all the amenities one needed for one's comfort. Naturally, the main

10   Five Minutes More

Four pictures of the Bette Davis birthday party. Upper left: WB teammates me, Joan Leslie and Jeffrey Lynn. Upper right: Me kissing Bette (note her throne). Lower left: With Ernest Borgnine. Lower right: Me and Cesar Romero.

reason was for the necessity of privacy for wardrobe changes in between scenes and for not having to leave the soundstage for when nature called.

As I explained in detail in my first book, my sister Anita was my mentor, my best friend, my mother figure, my all and was always by my side. However, when working on a movie and especially if one starred in that movie the studio assigned you a dresser.

Now if you picture some person helping you in and out of your jacket as their main task you would be doing a disservice to the true value of such a professional. I can only give you a simple example of how very important a dresser is to a movie production.

In my movie, *The Captain's Kid*, I had a scene where Guy Kibbee, Jane Bryan and I were digging for treasure on an island. The earth was quite damp and because I was kneeling into it with one knee it left a muddy imprint on the pants of my sailor suit. Of course, this was written into the script so wardrobe knew that I would require a duplicate outfit that was clean just in case we would have to reshoot a scene that took place *prior* to the digging for treasure. To be on the safe side there were always extra precautions entailed with something like that. The script girl wrote down the configuration of the stain so that it could be matched and, to cinch it, the still photographer took a close-up picture of it and that way nothing was left to chance. It may sound like a lot of work for such a simple scene but that's what made our movies so great. Happenstance was not tolerated.

Anita and I.

There were many other duties put on the shoulders of the dresser. Before anyone got to the set in the morning, it was up to her to bring down all of the scheduled changes for that day to the trailer and to make sure the garments were spotless and pressed to perfection.

It is a fact that being a dresser to a little girl would be simple in comparison to, say, a period costume movie starring Bette Davis.

Much to my excitement Bette Davis and I shared the same dresser. Her name was Little Ida and although she was not much taller than I, what a dynamo she was! Everyone on the Lot knew Little Ida. It was a fact that she could handle anything that came up in Wardrobe with ease and with no sense of panic. Although Miss Davis insisted on having her on all of her movies, if there was no conflict in our movie schedules, I then always got Little Ida. How wonderful that was for me because then I could pepper the poor dear with questions galore about my idol. Bless her heart, she had the patience of Job and answered all of my queries as best as she could. She got very used to me saying that perhaps one day I would have the opportunity of doing a movie with Miss Davis. Encouragingly, Ida would mention that that was a good possibility seeing that we both worked for the same studio. Of course, I never got tired of hearing that, but, alas, it never happened. But I did come close....two times. However, much occurred before those opportunities presented themselves.

I was a busy little girl in 1936. In the midst of making a movie called *The Captain's Kid,* with the adorable Guy Kibbee and the equally wonderful May Robson, for the first and last time in my career I worked on *two* productions at the same time.

On Sundays or any spare time that I wasn't working on *The Captain's Kid* (which was a rare occurrence because I was in it almost from start to finish), I was practicing a precision military tap routine for a Technicolor short subject that I was to star in called *The Changing of the Guard.*

To digress for just a moment, this short has a very interesting history that starts in 1936 and carries through to 70 years later. The premise of the story is that I am a little English girl living with her grandfather and his man servant who had been his aide in the army before they both retired from the service. It is now New Year's Eve and I ask my grandfather to repeat his story of the night of his celebratory dinner surrounded by all of his fellow officers who were bidding him a farewell on his retirement. This is a banquet scene and the men supposedly sing all of my grandfather's favorite Scottish songs, which is pre-empted by Scottish bagpipers marching around the table. The actual songs were pre-recorded by a magnificent men's choral group and the actors who played the officers merely mouthed the words.

This short, for many years, was shown every New Year's Eve in the theaters of all the countries under the British Empire. Nowadays, it is shown quite frequently on the Turner Classic Movies (TCM) and other venues and I am proud to say that it stands up in production values even in this day and age.

There is a dream sequence where I am regaled in kilts and plaids on the grounds of Buckingham Palace and I sing a song with two 6-foot British Guardsmen on each side of me. After the song concludes, a full troop of red-coated palace guards march and follow me into the main palace grounds. But, in this case, as they turn around to face the camera the "guardsmen" turn out to be crackerjack-perfect Busby Berkeley dancing girls who back me up in a precision military tap dance. What is incongruous about the whole thing is the short was directed by Bobby Connelly. At Warners, he was second in command as dance director, but it was Buzz who rehearsed me in my dance routine and Bobby who rehearsed the girls. The girls and I never rehearsed together and the first time we met was the day we shot the dance sequence. The "shoot" went as smoothly as silk and one would swear we had been rehearsing together for weeks!!

Another interesting fact attached to this short is that on Broadway, Mitzi Mayfair, the musical comedy star, starred in this same dance number in The *Daughter of the Regiment,* which was one of Florenz Ziegfield's last productions and it was directed by…Bobby Connelly!!

With Daniel Frohman and Bobby Connely.

Now to get back to the subject of how moviemaking, even for a child, can get hectic. The very same day we shot the dance sequence, and after I had a quick lunch, I had to get over to the set of *The Captain's Kid* to do an emotional scene in a jail cell with Guy Kibbee. (Watch for a showing of it on TCM.) It is a scene where I visit my Uncle Asa, who has been jailed for something he never did and we are to part because I am going out of town, back to my home away, from Stansburyport. The jail cell is all locked up and I want to say a real goodbye to Uncle Asa, whom I just idolize. Our chauffeur has a dubious past, but he has a soft spot for the child so he jimmies the lock so that she can say her goodbyes from inside the cell. While he is doing his "work" on the lock, I am observing what he is doing by stooping down on the floor and looking up at his handiwork. When the time comes and I am to be taken away from my hero, it is a highly emotional scene where I get hysterical at the thought of leaving Uncle Asa. Some reviewers of the movie (then and now) point to that scene as one of the best dramatic scenes ever displayed by a child in motion pictures.

However, here is a fact that even the director did not know at that time. When I looked up at the chauffeur jimmying the lock, a speck of steel had entered my eye and it was only after the director had called

"CUT" that anyone knew that I had an injury to my eye. Luckily, a quick trip to an eye specialist determined that there was no damage done and after the removal of the small speck I was sent home until the next day so that the red irritation in my eye could heal.

I did four Technicolor shorts for Warner Bros. and in the year 2006 one of them, *A Day at Santa Anita*, was featured as an "extra" on the new Jimmy Cagney DVD, *Each Dawn I Die*. All of the others, except my favorite, *The Changing of the Guard*, are also on various other DVDs as extras.

Just about all of my scenes from *A Day at Santa Anita* were shot at the actual track, which was only three years old at that time. But there was an insert that was done at the studio that featured my guest stars doing cameo bits supposedly taking place in the box seats at the track.

I visited the set when Al Jolson and Ruby Keeler were doing their scenes, but until I saw the finished product at the premier showing of the short I didn't know who the rest of the stars were …and what top flight stars they were!!

I remember the audience's intake of breath when the likes of Olivia de Havilland, Edward G. Robinson, Al and Ruby, Hugh Herbert, Frank McHugh, Allen Jenkins, Mary Treen and…Bette Davis made their

Ruby Keeler. Hugh Herbert and I in *A Day at Santa Anita*.

Ruby and me at the Palomino Club for charity.

appearances. I almost fell off my seat in the theater when Bette Davis came on. Although we didn't have a scene together, as far as I was concerned, we were in the same movie together!!! This was a dream come true, although I still had the hope that we really would be in a movie together some time in the future like Little Ida had predicted would happen.

Evelyn Keyes and me at the American Cinema Awards. She portrayed Ruby in *The Jolson Story*.

16 Five Minutes More

As a little side fact that bears repeating, I mentioned in *My Fifteen Minutes* that there were two other stars in the short doing a cameo bit, but Mr. Warner had released both of them from his contractee list because he didn't see too much of a future for either one of them and just didn't want to give them any more Warner Bros exposure. Their names? Virginia Bruce…and…Clark Gable!!

In the early 1980s the Film Advisory Board held a huge birthday party for Bette Davis and I was one of the fortunate people to have been put on the dais at that event. A lot of stars were seated at various tables and one by one, including those of us seated at the dais, got up on stage with Bette Davis, who very appropriately seated on a throne, and told some very interesting stories that involved Ms. Davis. Just about everyone spoke about the other stars she had appeared with, but when it got to my turn I mentioned the names of two people that I wished could have been there that night; two people that absolutely adored her. I spoke of Little Ida and the head gaffer that was on most of Miss Davis's and, incidentally, my movies, who went by the name of Ham. These stories took Miss Davis by surprise and I know she was genuinely touched by them. However, I also told her about how thrilled I was that she had had a cameo in my Technicolor short and how ecstatic I was when news had come through that I was to have played her daughter in a Warners movie in 1938. I prefaced my story by saying that due to her impeccable good taste in storylines and scripts, she refused to do the movie. She rose from her seat on the throne and genuinely was concerned that it might have mistakenly been seen that it had been because I was to have played her daughter, but I assured her that was not the reason. The truth was that that movie was the last straw for her and served as the perfect excuse for her to bring suit against Warner Bros. for various contract violations. She fled to Europe where the suit was eventually settled between Jack Warner and his star through the British courts and she returned to America and back to Warner Bros. I will write more about that movie that I did with another star as my mother in one of the following chapters in this book.

After that evening was over I received a beautiful letter from Miss Davis thanking me for my contribution in making her birthday party so memorable. On the night of her banquet I had given her a present of an original piece of sheet music from the movie *Now, Voyager,* but as a surprise she signed it and sent it back to me. I treasure it to this day.

A Potpourri of Talent   17

THERE IS NOTHING LIKE A DAME

In the movies of the thirties, the term "dame" was used affectionately to describe a woman who appeared to be hard as nails but actually had a heart of gold. At Warner Bros you can bet when a script came along with that description no casting call went out to fill that slot. It was almost written in stone that the part would go to either Glenda Farrell or Joan Blondell, depending on their availability.

This was an ideal situation for everyone involved and the two women knew that there was no need for jealousy when one or the other got the part. They were both down-to-earth ladies and because they were under contract to Warner Bros. they realized that the studio would keep each of them busier than most of the actresses in all of Hollywood.

What might surprise you is that I have devoted this chapter about dames not only to Glenda and Joan, but to two other actresses as well. One might think at first glance that they do *not* belong in this category.

However, I am judging this on my own personal experience and always thought that in real life their personalities were very similar.

So here goes. See if you agree with me at the end of the chapter. There was Joan Blondell, Glenda Farrell and…Marion Davies and Carole Lombard!! Of the four ladies I only worked with Glenda, but knew the others quite well socially.

When I first came to Warner Bros., I had done a very short scene with Dick Powell in *Broadway Gondolier*. When Jack Warner saw the daily of that particular scene, he made the decision to scrap it and instead to star me in *Little Big Shot*.

After the script was tailored to me and my various talents of mimicry and dancing and singing, casting for the rest of the characters were begun. In essence, it was a story about two "get-rich-quick schemers" that, at the beginning of the movie, reluctantly get stuck with a little girl who becomes orphaned after her father, a distant acquaintance of theirs, is shot and killed. The two men were played beautifully by Robert Armstrong and his cohort, the irrepressible Edward Everett Horton. Glenda Farrell, of course, played Armstrong's patient but tough "dame." We also had a bonanza of first-class "heavies" who figured prominently in the dramatic phase of the movie. How much better can you get than the gangster types who menaced all of us than J. Carrol Naish, Jack LaRue, Marc Lawrence, and Ward Bond? By the way, all of them were very nice gentlemen and nothing like the characters they habitually portrayed in the movies.

You must remember that I was new to this country and was a typical little English girl who found American accents fascinating. Starting when I was very young I was a good mimic and had a good ear for accents so therefore found Americans very diverse in their intonations and accents which I assumed, when I became an adult, stemmed from the states they originally came from. By the nature of the animal, one never knew for sure whether an actor's accent was his own or one that he assumed for a part or perhaps liked it so much that it eventually became part of his persona. As an example, look at Pat O'Brien, who on and off the screen was the epitome of *the* Irishman yet the true fact was he was born in Milwaukee, Wisconsin!!

I just recently read an older book written by my friend, the late Lana Turner, and she said that when she was making a movie with Spencer Tracy she came in one morning and before they started work for the day she started to chat with him. She had just finished a movie called *Green Dolphin Street*, in which she portrayed a British woman and the start of this new movie with Tracy was almost back to back with the other one and she was having trouble keeping her accents straight. As she chatted with the great actor he listened intently to what she was saying and when she paused for breath he looked at her with a trace of a smile on his face and said, "My, aren't we British this morning."

I was fascinated by Glenda Farrell's speech pattern. It was not so much so for the accent she used in our movie but because she had a decided lisp which I imagine stemmed from the fact that she had an enormous overbite. Funnily enough, her son, Tommy, also had an overbite but not to the extent that his mother did.

It's interesting how various actors react after a director calls CUT and ends the scene. They are either still "into their character" or they are extremely quiet and withdrawn or relieved that the shot was a good one. With Glenda it was another story. Sometimes I could hardly wait for the director to call CUT because you never knew what she was going to come up with. Not that it made her any less of an actress, but she assumed her own persona as soon as the scene ended and because she had a marvelous sense of humor with a quick wit to accompany it she could find something funny in the direst circumstances. Surprisingly enough, she was also very much the motherly type.

There is a scene in the movie where I am just devastated because one of the gangsters had kicked my little dog and it died. I am lying in bed barely able to talk from crying and gathered around me are the two men who have learned to love me. Lying in bed with me is Glenda's character who is trying to comfort me. It's a very emotional scene and after the director called CUT everyone was unusually quiet. Both Bob Armstrong and Edward E. patted my hand and left the set, but Glenda remained and cuddled me in her arms. This was the gentle Glenda and not her character reacting to me.

Usually when a movie is completed you and your fellow actors part company, go your separate ways, and then onto your next assignment. With Glenda it was quite different. She kept my adored elder sister Anita and me in her life and we were regularly invited to her home for dinners and lunches and it became a tradition to always go to her house on the Fourth of July. She arranged for a fireworks display in her backyard that could have competed with most of the exhibits we see at our public parks of today. Very child-like she would get as awed and excited with each display that lit up the sky as the youngest guest in her home. Much to the delight of all of us she never served "sophisticated" food on this holiday but made sure that there was a bountiful supply of "junk food," which she enjoyed as much as anyone there. This was Glenda's personality and which endeared her to all of us who were lucky enough to be in her inner circle.

I always regretted not reuniting with her when I returned to America right after the end of World War II. It was not for the want of trying, I assure you. You see, at that time, contract lists no longer existed at most of the top studios and it was hard to find where everyone was now living. Many of the stars bought homes out of state and only came into town when there was a job to do or they became gypsies. Gypsies were actors who were no longer under contract to one studio but worked at most of them when parts became available to them. It was also very hard to track them down for a number of reasons and some of the reasons were very sad considering these were experienced actors. Work was no longer plentiful and a lot of agents arbitrarily dropped them as clients and, instead, pushed for their newer and younger actors. Also, in the past, if all else failed, one could always write a letter to them in care of the Screen Actors Guild and it would be forwarded on to them, but the Guild did away with that service years ago.

In the eighties I did manage to get in touch with Tommy who, at that time was doing double duty as an actor and selling foreign cars. Much to my sadness, he told me that Glenda had passed away in 1971 at the too early age of sixty-six.

In Africa, during the war, I remember going to see the movie *Johnny Eager*, starring my friend Lana Turner and I was extremely touched and impressed with the beautiful performance that Glenda turned in that movie. Far afield of her usual "good dame" characters, and although the part was very small, she was unforgettable as a widow down on her luck. She made the most of what little they gave her. The very next time it comes on television do take note of her performance.

Glenda truly loved acting and was one of the easiest people to relate to in a scene because she not only cared about *her* character she also cared about *yours*!

At a Screen Actors Guild special meeting. I represented the '30s and '40s. The "kids" behind me are ex-TV child stars.

In person, Joan Blondell was much more attractive than she appeared in films. She had beautiful expressive blue eyes and a knockout figure. As young as I was, I could tell that men were attracted to her like bees to honey and it was as much for her beauty as it was for her sense of humor and innate intelligence. She, too, had an enthusiasm for life.

I remember vividly the first time we met and what she said to me, saying it with a perfectly straight face, "Are you married?" As a little English girl who took everything literally, my jaw almost dropped to the ground because *no one* had ever asked me something like that! She again tried. "Well, maybe not married but perhaps engaged?" By looking at the expressions of the faces of the people that surrounded us, I finally got an inkling she was kidding me. When I started to smile at her, she suddenly scooped me up in her arms and gave me a big bear hug. That was typical of Joan. Kidding one moment, warm and loving the next.

It was rather strange to me as a kid because somehow I felt wives and husbands stayed together forever, but I just happened to know both of her husbands from her earlier marriages.

In 1936 I was co-starring in a movie with the great Al Jolson called *The Singing Kid* and our cinematographer was George Barnes who, at that time, was married to Joan. I never saw her come to the set or on location where other wives and husbands visited, but that must have been because she and Mr. Barnes were either separated or even divorced by then.

However, her next husband, Dick Powell, I knew very well. (Read about him in *My Fifteen Minutes.*) When they were married in 1936, I saw a lot of both of them on the studio lot. As a matter of fact, when the Prince and Princess of Spain were on their honeymoon and Warner Bros. hosted their stay when they were in Hollywood, the studio asked the royal couple whom they would like to meet. I was one of the lucky ones who were chosen and they both attended my 6th birthday party. Or to be correct I should have said my birthday *parties*. The first one was a rather informal celebration held in the studio café that was used strictly by the stars and executives at Warner Bros. called the Green Room. Attending the luncheon was one of my favorite directors Mervyn LeRoy; Dick Powell, who was dressed in a tuxedo because he was in the middle of shooting a movie; Joan, who was just visiting the Lot that day; my sister Anita and my uncle; a few Warner executives and the Princess of Bourbon of Spain. However, that evening my birthday party was a very formal affair attended by both of the royal couple and many of the studios' top stars.

A humongous cake was brought in at the end of the dinner and after I blew out the candles and everyone sang a rousing happy birthday to me, the cake was cut and the first slices I handed to the Prince and Princess. Many pictures were taken and in 2004 I sent copies of them to their son, the present King of Spain, Juan Carlos. He sent a most gracious letter expressing his gratitude and affection for me for sending him these pictures that he had never seen of his parents on their honeymoon in Hollywood and he autographed a beautiful regal photo of himself which I treasure to this day.

Like most of us under contract to a studio, I had occasion to see Joan quite a lot at the studio and at various functions even though we never worked together. We would often talk about her handsome husband Dick Powell because she knew what a really big crush I had on him and she teased me that he wore my scarf every day whether it was hot or cold weather.

You see, I had learned to knit in England when I was four years old by my grandmother and when I was making my first movie at Warners I spent my time knitting a scarf for him. It was so long in length it could have gone around the necks of three men with room to spare. When I had finished work on the scarf, my sister Anita had it beautifully gift wrapped and to this day I don't know whether Dick was amazed and amused at the size and "design" of the garment that were knit in red, white and blue squares or just taken aback that a five-year-old took the time to knit this for him. I remember that Joan was there when I presented the present to Dick and tears just welled up in her eyes. They were both very loving and took turns giving me kisses and hugs. In my first book, I tell a rather poignant tale of our relationship all the way up to the time when I had my last communication with Dick when he became terminally ill with cancer. Sadly, by that time, Joan was out of his life and he was now married to June Allyson.

As I have mentioned previously, it didn't matter whether you were a child or an adult, if you were under contract to Warners you appeared at every preview of a Warners movie whether you were in it or not. Many a time I sat next to Joan in the theater and for me that was total fun because she would whisper naughty things in my ears as the picture progressed. My dear sister warned me not to giggle out loud no matter what Joan said to me and believe me that was a hard thing to do. Don't let me give you the wrong impression. She *never* said anything obscene. She just said funny things that a child wished that they *could* say…but didn't dare!!

I was very sad when I heard that she and Dick were no longer married. They really did seem like an ideal couple but, of course, I saw them through a child's idealistic eyes.

A strange little footnote. June Allyson and I looked *nothing* alike when I was a child with pitch black hair and a Dutch bob. However, as adults, we looked startlingly similar and were often taken for each other out in public.

I often wonder nowadays what Dick would have thought had he seen fairly recent pictures of her and me together!!

Mr. William Randolph Hearst, the newspaper mogul, had a motion picture production company called Cosmopolitan. For the most part it was used to produce movies starring his lady love, Marion Davies. She was not a great actress, but a very good comedienne and those were the type of movies she excelled in. I'm not quite sure why Mr. Hearst moved his production company from one site to Warner Bros., but I don't think anyone will ever forget the day that Miss Davies' "dressing room" was moved to our Lot. That so-called dressing room was the size of a full three-bedroom house and was suited out with the best of furnishings that was fit for a queen. Well, in a way she *was* a queen.

Although Mr. Hearst was a married man, Marion was the love of his life and there wasn't anything he wouldn't do for her. Funnily enough, her needs were simple. Just like the two other ladies in this chapter, she was warm, outgoing and very child-like as well. Other than the fact that she was a beautiful-looking woman I think that was what was very appealing to Mr. Hearst, who, at times, almost treated her like an adored daughter and who tried to continually surprise her with things she delighted in. Maybe it was because I was a child, but I remember him as a very tall man and the thing that impressed me the most about him was his tummy. It looked like one could ski down it!!

As far as I could see he was a quiet man around her and *very* conservative. I think he left all of the demonstrative highs of life's emotions to his lady love and just stood back and admired her. There isn't much about her he didn't approve of . . . except one thing. He did not like her drinking any alcohol. One thing I remember quite distinctly about Marion is she wore beautiful clothes, lovely perfume, but if you got up to her close enough there was no doubt that there was liquor on her breath. I never saw her drunk and I attended a few of her parties at her magnificent home in Santa Monica. Sober, she was happy. Imbibing, she was even happier!! It really was just a matter of degrees, but Mr. Hearst didn't even approve of that because it was obvious that her love-of-life attitude was exacerbated when she had indulged in liquor. When I was an adult, I had heard that up at Hearst Castle, when many luminaries were invited to stay for weekends, no liquor was served at meal times. That bothered none of the guests because they knew that if they ever wanted a drink, there was plenty stashed away in various hiding places in Marion's suite. Apparently, her suite was quite a distance away from Mr. Hearst's so he never heard the parties that went on well into the mornings.

The very first time I ever met Marion was in the Green Room at Warners. I had learned Parisian French when I was just a tot and one day at lunch we were served by a new waitress who had just come from her home in Paris. I had fun talking to her in her native tongue and even ordered my lunch in French. Marion overheard this and came over to our table. She asked my sister Anita, "Just how old is this child?" and when Anita told her she smiled and said in a very loud voice that must have been heard by everyone in the restaurant "When I was her age I had just barely learned how to say Mama!" Two days later that appeared in the newspaper and I can see it quite readily in one of my scrapbooks to this day.

Marion liked Anita and me quite a lot and invited us to lunch in her dressing room quite often. She was fascinated about learning about South Africa because nine times out of ten, in those days, the general public pictured *all* of Africa as a jungle.

To digress for just a moment, many years ago when I was a young adult, the late Laurence Harvey and I bemoaned the fact that every time a travelogue was shown about South Africa it stayed exclusively with Kruger National Park and certainly not on the modern cities, the beautiful mountains, the pristine beaches of Cape Town, Johannesburg and Durban. In 2007, I am *still* waiting for a decent representation of modern Africa to be shown on a travelogue.

Now to get back to Marion and Randolph Hearst.

He had gifted Marion with quite a number of homes and although I had never been to her Beverly Hills home I certainly had to her huge home in Santa Monica. It was so big that had it not been on beach property it would have taken up a minimum of a city block. As it was, it took up quite an acreage of the Pacific Coast Highway. Many years later when it was sold, it was turned into a private hotel and club and today a minuscule part of the original house still exists.

I remember a particularly fun time I had at the beach house. It was a costume ball and everyone was supposed to come as someone from a famous book, poem, play or painting. Everyone was in costume except Mr. Hearst. I must say he *did* make a small effort by wearing a cowboy hat. If I remember correctly Marion came as Marie Antoinette and I was very excited because I got to dress up as Mary who had a little lamb. I had a toy lamb that was attached to wheels so that when I pulled the leash it would follow me.

Needless to say that the jewels that Marion wore that night were real and for good reason Mr. Hearst looked very nervous that she would lose one of them as she enthusiastically danced the night away. Other than that he seemed very amused observing the costumes everyone was wearing. Although no prizes were given for the best costume, we all got baskets filled with various goodies to commemorate the occasion. Because I was a young child Anita and I left quite early, but the very next day at the studio Marion said that I had looked adorable and she hoped that we had had a good time.

I think that was the last time that I saw Marion, but I never forgot how very nice she was to me.

Now for the last star on this list of DAMES.

By now the reader must know that in the thirties the movie colony attended many benefits. The young people of this era believe that they started this trend but long before they or their parents were born we put a great effort into improving the lives of those less fortunate. I must say, regardless of the era, it is still a most worthwhile and humane thing to do and I applaud all who take the time and effort to do so.

When I was still under contract to Warners, Anita and I got to meet a very nice lady at a benefit we all attended in Bel Air. It was held on the grounds of the estate of a very wealthy couple. The man was an industrialist and his wife was from generations of the social register, but they weren't snobs as one would imagine. They not only hosted many a benefit but donated heavily to all of them.

The crème de la crème of Hollywood attended that afternoon and because a familiar circuit of stars usually attended these events Anita and I had met most of them.

That particular day we were talking to Claudette Colbert when a nice-looking woman joined us. Apparently, she was a good friend of Miss Colbert's and after they greeted each other we were introduced to her. I remember quite vividly that the star called her friend "Fieldsie" and when she heard my name she was most complimentary about my work at Warner Bros. and mentioned that she and her husband had seen just about all of them. She was curious as to what my next movie would be and, if I remember correctly, it was a time when I was just about to start the filming of *The Great O'Malley*, in which Humphrey Bogart portrayed my father.

Fieldsie seemed to be very popular because many people stopped by our little group to greet her and she always made sure that Anita and I were introduced to those we had never met before. Later, when we got to know this lady a little bit better, we found out she did a lot of nice things for a lot of people. That was just her generous nature.

Many months had gone by before we met her again. It was at another benefit, but this time it took place at the famous Shrine Auditorium. As was usual, all the stars participating in the event were gathered backstage waiting their turn to go on stage and pitch for donations for that particular cause. Anita and I were waiting near the wings when who should approach us with a bright smile and warm greeting but Fieldsie. She said that only a few nights ago she and her husband were talking about me and what a fine little actress I was. I thanked her very much and told her how much I truly loved acting. She asked Anita and me whether we would like to come to tea at her house one day that was convenient to all of us and, of course, we said that we would indeed. By the time we exchanged addresses and phone numbers she had to excuse herself because she had to get back to her best friend to help her get ready for the show. It was very crowded backstage and although Anita and I tried to see who Fieldsie's friend was we didn't have much luck because people were pretty well meshed in together and all we could make out was that her friend had blonde hair.

About a week later we got a phone call from Fieldsie asking Anita and me whether we would like to visit Paramount studios to meet her friend the next day for lunch. The shooting of *The Great O'Malley* had not yet begun so for the first time in ages I was free, but Anita had a business appointment with my agent and couldn't make it. Our new friend assured Anita that I would be well taken care of and be supervised at all times and returned safely back home after meeting her best friend who apparently worked for Paramount studios. After Anita okayed the get-together the very next day Fieldsie called for me at home and gave Anita a phone number at Paramount where she could reach us at any time on that day.

I knew enough about security at studios to know that my new adult friend was well known enough at the studio to be let in immediately by the studio gate man. Although I had
been a visitor to Universal, MGM and the Hal Roach studios in the past this was my first time on the Paramount Lot and I found it very interesting.

I could hardly wait to see who it was that was Fieldsie's best friend. Imagine my surprise and delight when we entered a beautiful dressing room to see that it was none other than the beautiful star Carole Lombard!! It was an extra special treat to find out how very down to earth she was and just as sweet as her friend Fieldsie!! It was late morning and she had a devilish grin on her face as she apologized for talking with her mouth full and that she didn't have any goodies left to share with me. You see, she had been indulging in a candy bar and Fieldsie laughingly told me not to follow in Carole's footsteps for it was a disastrous habit to be eating candy for breakfast!!

I must admit that I had one uncomfortable moment. Both ladies insisted that I call them by their first names and I had been brought up to call adults by Mr. Mrs. or Miss and if the relationship was very close, Aunt or Uncle. Anything other than that showed a lack of respect. However, those were Carole and Fieldsie's wishes so I hesitantly complied.

We did not go to the Paramount dining room for lunch because Carole was going to be working later on and she felt more at ease ordering in so that we could get better acquainted. She, too, was very interested in hearing all about South Africa and mentioned that a boyfriend of hers would surely like to go there one day and hunt wild animals. (Did she perhaps mean Clark Gable?) She found it quite amusing when I told her that neither my family nor my friends had ever been on a safari and the only animals that we had ever seen was at our local zoos.

Carole was a great audience and had a ready and infectious laugh that came loud and often!!! It was getting around the time for lunch and she asked me if there was anything special that I wanted to eat or should she just order for all of us. I smiled to myself thinking that if this lady liked candy bars for breakfast what might she order for lunch!! I opted for her ordering the lunch.

I was really puzzled when Fieldsie started putting a checkered tablecloth on the floor! She noticed that I looked at her in a puzzling manner, but she just smiled and explained that Carole adored picnics and if she couldn't eat outdoors she would have her picnics indoors. I thought that was such a wonderful idea and even more so because it came from a grownup!

The lunch itself was quite an adventure and when it was over and Fieldsie took up the tablecloth I was very surprised when Carole asked me to stay down on the floor with her. When she said that she had a favor to ask of me I wondered what a child could possibly do for a grownup movie star. It was not long in coming.

"Do you know how to play Jacks?"

I wasn't quite sure what she meant until she described the game to me.

I said, "Oh, you mean onceys twoseys. Yes, I know how to play it."

She asked me to teach her and before I knew it Fieldsie had placed all of the pieces necessary for the game on the floor.

It took Carole a while to get used to picking up more than two jacks at a time and she would roll over and laugh each time she missed, but after an hour or so she started getting the hang of it.

When Fieldsie reluctantly broke up the game because it was time for her friend to go to work Carole gave me a huge hug and told me what a delight it was having me over for a short while and that she hoped that we would see each other again very soon. Unfortunately, that was not to be. You can imagine how I felt when I heard years later that Carole and her mother had died in a plane crash coming back to California after a war bond tour. I was so privileged to have met a very fine lady who never forgot her friends. That was evident when it came out that in her will she left just about everything to Fieldsie.

It's a funny thing, but I could never figure out why Carole wanted to learn how to play Jacks. The closest thing I could get to it was when

The Blue Bird.

A Potpourri of Talent

Rare shot that was edited out of *The Blue Bird*. Inside the house of Angela Berlingto who suddenly discovers she can walk!

Anita suggested that maybe she had to learn how to do it for a part in a movie. Many, many years later when I was relating this story to my friend Roddy McDowall he started laughing. He cleared the mystery up by informing me that in the thirties a favorite parlor game with the stars was called Strip Jax. Each time you failed to pick up your designated number of jacks you had to strip off a piece of your clothing. I smiled to myself that I hoped that Carole got in a little more practice before she tried it out on her friends!!

I am sure by now you see how very much alike all these fabulous ladies were. As I understand it, all of them retained their child-like enthusiasm till the day that they died and I only hope that somehow they sensed how much they had meant to a young child who was in awe of them. As I reminisce now, I wouldn't have traded one second of any of those memories for anything in the world.

Just a little addendum to this story.

I did see Fieldsie again after that day at Paramount. She had invited Anita and me to her home in Beverly Hills where we also met her charming husband. They both gave us a tour of their beautiful home and their back garden was just like something out of England. Lots of manicured lawn with brilliant patches of flowers and iron benches painted white where one could just relax and read a book. I liked Fieldsie's husband right away and even at my young age I could see how very right they were for each other. From his conversation at tea time I gathered that at one time he had been an actor, but decided that he would enjoy directing even better and then actively pursued that goal from thereon in.

About a year and a half later my contract with Warners was up. I almost immediately got signed to do one outside movie, *Woman Doctor*. Lucky for me, before we got midway through that production, two studios offered to sign me to a contract after my obligation to *Woman Doctor* was finished. The studios were MGM and Twentieth Century-Fox. I don't know what made my agent choose Fox over MGM, but I have a feeling that the money that was offered was his deciding factor.

As everyone knows, the first picture that I was assigned to at Fox was the production of *The Little Princess* and after that *The Blue Bird*. Both movies starred Shirley Temple and both movies were directed by Walter Lang…Fieldsies's husband!!

ERIN GA BRAUGH

"M'darlin', if the Irish and the English got along half as well as you and I do, aaal would be right in the world." I was not quite nine years old when my dear friend Pat O'Brien said this to me during the making of our Warner Bros movie, *The Great O'Malley*.

I personally cannot think of another human being who so epitomized everything that is great about the Irish more than Pat did. One of his many virtues that I loved the most was the one of loyalty. He was intense about that and if he was your friend, you had a friend for life. As I mentioned in my first book, *The Great O'Malley* was fraught with difficulties strictly due to our director's personality quirks. There is no argument that the man was a first-class director. After all, one only has to look up his credits to see how well he helmed some of the greatest motion pictures of that era, but undoubtedly he just did not like actors of any age or sex. Because I was a child, I was not exempt from his Teutonic attitudes. I mentioned this story in my last book, but it bears repeating so that one can get an idea what goes on on some movie sets.

In this movie I portrayed the crippled daughter of Humphrey Bogart and Frieda Inescort. The Phillips family was down on their luck and lived on the East Side of New York in a dismal little apartment. The father had been out of work for a long time but on this particular day he was on his way to start on his first day of work at a

An "intimate and emotional" scene from *The Great O'Malley*. The man in the white shirt in front is Oscar-winning cinematographer Ernie Haller.

factory. Officer O'Malley (Pat O'Brien) had the reputation of being an unrelenting police officer who carried out the law "by the book" and even his superiors were slowly starting to lose their patience with him. On this day O'Malley stops Phillips to give him a ticket for a noisy muffler and makes him late for his new job. The job is given to someone else and in desperation the father takes his war medals to a hock shop to get some money for them but an argument ensues and he accidentally shoots the man behind the counter. To make a long story short O'Malley gets demoted to a school crossing guard when the father is sent to jail and O'Malley, coincidentally, gets acquainted and is "humanized" by his eventual love for the little crippled girl and her school teacher played by Ann Sheridan.

Our first shooting date for the start of the movie was delayed because our director, William Dieterle, and his wife based their lives on the pseudoscience of astrology and unless the planets were all in alignment they felt uneasy starting any project. That was for starters. In fact, when he was first assigned to our movie, he did not want to do it for many reasons which I won't go into again. It is obvious he carried his resentment over to all of us that were connected to the production and apart from giving scene directions he isolated himself from all of us.

I must preface my story with a little information that you need to know. If you will look at any movie or photograph that I was in up till this time you will see that I was never without a gold bangle on my wrist. This was a tradition and all of us girls in my family wore this piece of jewelry. By the time I was nine the bangle fit nicely on my wrist; however, if I wanted to take it off it would have had to be cut off.

William Dieterle suddenly became aware of it and gave orders to my sister to take it off my wrist as I was supposed to be a poor girl. My sister Anita was a very gentle type of person and she tried to explain the situation to him, but he was having nothing to do with any explanations and ordered the bangle to be cut off my wrist. He did it in such a harsh manner that Bogey spoke up and said, "For chrissake, Bill, the girl could have bought that at a dime store. It ain't that important!" That's all our director had to hear. He angrily stomped off the set to get to the nearest phone and called Mr. Warner to complain. Apparently, Mr. Warner agreed with Bogie's estimation for I was allowed to keep the bangle on. I think everyone in the cast had their difficulties with Mr. Dieterle and that continued on till the very last day of shooting.

Throughout this movie Pat was my champion. He was so very sensitive to people's feelings and although he didn't verbalize too much he showed how much he cared through many generous gestures. It was one day after a particularly rough time the day before that I had from our director that I found a little wrapped present in my dressing room. It was a lovely gold chain bracelet that one puts charms on. By the time of the last day of shooting *The Great O'Malley*, that bracelet was filled with significant charms gifted to me by Pat. At night he would tell Eloise, his lovely wife of many years, what a particular problem had occurred that day and she would go out and shop for a charm that would just make "everything right." I adored Pat. He loved to sing and he knew more Irish folk songs than anyone I ever knew. You never had to coax him to sing and he often did that between scenes just to ease the heavy atmosphere.

In mid-1938 my contract was up at Warners. It wasn't a shock to us because a lot of people were being let go because of a generalized economic sweep. It wasn't too long before stars like Kay Francis and Pat were let go. Even though Anita and I were close to the whole O'Brien clan I didn't see them until World War II was over and I was back in America.

But before that happened I have an amusing story to tell you. Pat and a bunch of other stars were on a worldwide personal appearance tour and, if memory serves me correctly, it must have been some time around mid-1947. When the group got to South Africa Pat was interviewed on the SABC (South African Broadcasting Corporation) and mid-interview Pat said he wanted to say something personal to a special Capetonian. The interviewer was delighted that Pat had something to say on a personal level and gave him the go-ahead.

"Sybil, m'darlin' I am now in your beautiful country and in your hometown…please do get in touch with me. I'd love to hear from you."

Well, the incongruity of this was that I had just arrived back in California and was no longer in South Africa and here was Pat in the place of my birth way across the world from the USA. My sister Anita got in touch with Pat immediately and told him that I was back in America. By the time Pat got back to Southern California Tony and I had just that week moved to a new place and the address and phone number that Anita had given to him was now obsolete. That didn't stop Pat and he got in touch with the top showbiz reporter, Louella Parsons, who, fortunately, had my update. It was thrilling to hear Pat's voice again and it was like no time had elapsed since we last had seen each other. We made arrangements for Tony and me to spend the day with him and Eloise at their home in Brentwood, just down the street from Shirley Temple's home, in the next week. I could hardly wait for the days to go by.

Their home reminded me of Scarlett O'Hara's home, Tara. It was a huge home consisting of 12 bedrooms, 14 bathrooms and a fantastic sewing room for Eloise. There was a lovely pool in the back with a pool house and a marvelous tennis court.

Pat didn't waste any time as soon as we came through the door. After some big hugs and welcoming kisses and introductions of Tony to my dear friends, Pat led me over to the bar area, where he made me sign my name and later on that was burnt into the bar. I remember my name was right next to Jimmy Cagney's!! What a wonderful day we had. Eloise gave me a tour of her huge-size sewing room and the project she was now in the middle of doing, and also a quick look into the O'Brien kids' rooms. By the time we women got ourselves updated with "girl talk" it was time to go downstairs and have lunch.

Pat also had another guest who came later that day. While he had been in Hong Kong, he had become friends with the mayor of that town and Pat had mentioned that the mayor and his family would be welcome in Pat's home any time they were in America. That day I had the pleasure of meeting the mayor's son and we all bonded very quickly. I told him of how much I enjoyed being in Hong Kong in 1941 and he found that fact fascinating and told me that as soon as he got home he would mention that to his father.

After his visit to Pat's home was over, the O'Briens asked Tony and me to stay over for dinner. It was still light outside and even though I had high heels on and stockings, I took my shoes off and played badminton with Pat on the tennis court.

Nothing like being a sophisticated married lady!!!!

That was such a delightful day and Tony and Pat got along so beautifully. Both men liked to lift a glass or two and that bonded them quicker than anything else!! And talking about lifting a glass or two of the "good stuff" (as Pat would call it) reminds me of the next time I saw Pat.

A huge party was given to stars of the past at the famous Lucy Restaurant near Paramount Studios and the evening was sponsored by

Mary Pickford. All the media, including television, covered it so our arrivals were very important. However, when Tony and I got there we went into the side entrance instead of coming in the front door and therefore weren't covered by the press. Coincidentally, Pat had done the same thing and being the show business star that he was he took hold of my arm and said, "Let's make our entrance where we should have in the first place. After all, that's the reason we're here." That was Pat for you. Never missed a trick!

But the clearest memory that I have of him that night still makes me laugh even as I write this. It came about when we got back to the bar area to join Tony once again. My husband ordered me a cocktail; he asked Pat what he would like to drink and then ordered a drink for himself. When our drinks came, Pat asked Tony to taste his glass of wine, a drink that was very strange and unusual for him to order. When Tony tasted it, Pat asked him what he thought of it. Only after Tony approved of it did Pat start drinking it. He must have sensed that Tony and I were quite puzzled about the whole thing. Pat was *not* a wine drinker!! Being the good Catholic that Pat was, he said, like it was the most natural thing on earth, "I gave up the hard stuff for Lent"!!

We kept in touch with the O'Briens throughout the years, but mostly by Christmas and birthday cards and telephone calls. All of our lives and schedules one way or the other had changed drastically and there really was no time for regular get-togethers. I now had a husband and baby and house to look after and all of the other things that involve a lifetime, yet even so, the love between us and the O'Briens never faded away.

One day I got a call from Pat and he said he was going into the hospital for a hernia operation. No big deal and said that after it was all over it would be nice if Tony and I came to the house when he was back home. I assured him we certainly would and if he preferred it we would even come to the hospital. He told us that wasn't necessary because it was a simple operation and he'd be home before we'd know it.

Well, I had a girlfriend that owned her own flower shop and I got an idea into my head, but I had to call up Pat's doctor before I could follow through with it. When I told the doctor what I planned to do but needed his permission, he gave a good hearty laugh and told me by all means to send Pat the present that I had in mind. I had my girlfriend make up a basket *not* of flowers but had her load it up with miniature bottles of Scotch and Whisky and all of the beverage goodies Pat liked the best. She said that she would get it out to the hospital within the next day or so.

I had been teaching kids' drama at the famous show business club The Masquers of Hollywood and producing and directing plays that we put on starring the kids. The next morning of the day of Pat's scheduled operation, I was deep in rehearsals with my students on stage and a rather unusual thing was happening.

A group of the board members of the Masquers had gathered in a little circle and it seemed to me they kept on glancing up at us on the stage. I was too busy and concentrating on the kids too much to notice that anything was amiss so I just continued on with our rehearsals. After a while I called a break and came off the stage to join my fellow board members. They sat me down on a chair and gently broke the news to me that Pat had just died at the hospital. All I could do was just shake!! Not a word came out of my mouth. I must have gone into shock for a few moments because everyone was trying to get me to say something and that wasn't happening. Finally, I came to and told them I had to get home. At that time Tony and I lived not too far away from the Masquers and I didn't even bother driving home. I ran!! As soon as I got in the front door I reached for the phone and called Pat's home. Mavourneen answered. She was Pat's oldest girl and the one I knew best and to this day I feel so ashamed how I broke down in tears to a child who had just lost her beloved father. I must say she was very calm and so mature for her age and instead of me comforting her she told me how much her dad thought of me. Apparently, Pat died of a heart attack during that simple operation and sadly nothing that they tried could bring him back.

About six months later I was a guest in the audience of a television show and who should be sitting right next to me but Brigid, the baby of the O'Brien family. Brigid looked so much like me when she was little and I could still see some of that resemblance even on that evening at the television station.

I am glad of one thing. Several years back, my daughter, Toni, just happened to be working on the Mike Douglas television show behind the scenes and she told Mike who her mother was. Seeing that Pat was one of his guest stars that day, he asked Toni if I could possibly manage to get down to the studio as soon as possible so that I could surprise Pat on camera.

Could I! You bet!!

On camera, when Mike was interviewing Pat, he stopped and said that there was a good friend and co-star of Pat's in the audience and asked if that someone would please stand up. Pat looked around with interest to see who that could be and when the television light hit me Pat came off the stage and got into the audience where the camera followed him and gave me a big hug. That was the last time Pat and I were on camera together. What a very special gentleman and friend he was. Eloise joined Pat not too long after his passing and I'd like to think that they are now living happily in their heavenly Tara.

THE PLEASURE OF HER COMPANY

When I first came to Warner Bros., after Jack Warner brought me over from England, there is no doubt who was queen of the lot. It was the beautiful Kay Francis.

It was 1935 and I had just starred in *Little Big Shot* and, thankfully, both the movie and I had been well received. As yet I had not been assigned my next movie, but the studio kept me busy doing all of the necessary things that would help advance my American career.

One morning I had to come into the studio very early for an all day photographic session that the publicity department had ordered. Those photos were to be used when the media wanted photos for stories that they would be running on me. Also, doing double duty, they were to be sent out to the fans that had written to me in care of the studio asking for an autographed picture.

Now that we are on this subject I am going to take this opportunity to answer a question I am asked on a regular basis.

Due to the vast numbers of letters that came into the studio it would have been impossible for me or any other actor to have signed the pictures individually. Once the photo was okayed for distribution I would come in and sign the picture just once and then they would be reproduced by the thousands. I am sure most of you will be very disappointed to also find out that very rarely does the star read their fan mail. There was a special department where studio personnel would read the letters that were sent to the star and the studio would respond to these requests. However, these readers would also determine if some of the letters were very special for various reasons and would then send those to my home to get special attention. We would take care of them ourselves usually with a letter and/or a personally inscribed photo. I understand that fan mail in this day and age is handled approximately in the same way.

My friend Shirley Temple also signed her photos just once, but when it came to the specially handled letters that were sent onto her home, those photos were usually signed by her mother, Gertrude Temple. Not long ago, when Shirley and I were having a phone conversation, I mentioned that I still had the autographed photo of herself that she signed to me many years ago. She asked me if I was sure that it was her signature and not her mother's and I assured her that she had signed that photo in front of me.

On this particular morning in 1935 and in the middle of my photographic session, a studio messenger delivered a large and heavy brown envelope to my sister Anita. Much to our excitement it contained the script and general information about my next movie assignment. I was to play the daughter of Kay Francis and it was going to be directed by the young genius Mervyn LeRoy. The movie was called *I Found Stella Parish* and it had a terrific assembly of actors. Playing Miss Francis's love interest was an actor who, like me, also came from Cape Town South Africa, Ian Hunter, and adding to the cast was actor Paul Lukas and the fine character actress Jesse Ralph.

It is always an exciting time on the very first day on the set to shoot a new movie. The set decorators, lighting experts, sound engineers, prop men, gaffers, script girl, makeup and wardrobe personnel, cinematographer and director usually have arrived before the actors to weave their various expertise so that everything is in readiness for a full day's "shoot." Hopefully when the actors arrive they come in fully prepared in costume, make-up and knowing their lines scheduled for that day.

There is another person I forgot to mention that is required by law to be on the set at all times to tutor a child under the age of 16 years of age. Luckily, I had the same teacher, Miss Lois Horn, the entire time I was under contract to Warner Bros and she became a very good friend of my sister Anita's and me. The law required a minimum of three hours of school work done by the child every working day and there was a rather complicated way of accomplishing this feat and a feat it was! For instance, say I was called into a scene at 9:11 a.m. and didn't finish until 9.40 a.m. My teacher would clock me out at

9.11 a.m. and then clock me in at 9:40 a.m. Perhaps I only got in 15 minutes of school time before I was called onto the set again. These were all added up by midday and hopefully by then I had at least 1½ hours in by then. This was all repeated until my three hours had been reached.

One time when Shirley Temple and I were doing *The Little Princess* the school teacher stopped production because by the time midday had been reached we had only wracked up an hour of schoolwork. Legally, she had every right to do that but it proved to be very expensive for the studio. We were the only two actors scheduled for scenes the rest of the day and they couldn't "shoot around us."

It's been my personal experience that most of the time one doesn't get to meet the cast and the director until the first morning "shoot" of the new movie. I'm sure it's quite different for the adults who work regularly at their studio. Many times, such as in the case of Miss Francis, she has worked numerous times with the same leading man or was very familiar on a personal or professional basis with the rest of the cast and or director. The first day on *I Found Stella Parish* was an eye opener for me. Already seated for our "round table conference" was our director, Mervyn LeRoy, who had an extremely endearing quality which, of course, put everyone at ease. Anita and I sat at two of several directors chairs ready to receive instructions for the day. By this time all the major adult actors had arrived and joined us.

Anita heard my intake of breath and looked over at me to see if I was all right. She saw that I was staring wide-eyed at Kay Francis. You see, by this time my sister and I had been away from our home and our family for about a year and a half but as soon as I saw Miss Francis, it was like seeing our own mother walk onto the set. The similarities in features were amazing. My mother was tall like Kay (I didn't inherit any height from her, unfortunately) and had pitch black hair even down to the widow's peak. The big difference was in the color of their eyes. My mother's eyes were very dark brown, but Miss Francis's were blue grey. We were very diplomatic in my immediate family. My sister Anita and our brother David got their dark eyes from our mother, and our eldest sister Ada and I got our blue eyes from our dad.

I knew that playing Kay Francis's daughter would not be hard for me to do. That was especially the case in one of the scenes where I haven't seen my mother for a long time and I ask tearfully if it is because she is lost or just doesn't want me anymore. The tears in that scene came very easily.

This particular movie set was a very pleasant one. As I had mentioned previously, our director was a sensitive and compassionate director who seemed to bring out the best in all of us. Anita and I loved talking to Ian Hunter about Cape Town and he thoroughly enjoyed being updated about our mutual hometown.

Paul Lukas was a very nice man, but didn't socialize much. Although he had a very intense personality, he did enjoy and appreciate jokes and funny stories and his serious face would light up delightfully when he heard a good tale.

Kay Francis amazed me in so many different ways.

For instance, I loved her laugh. The best way I could describe it would be that it was loud…*very* loud and it sounded like she had a case of bronchitis which, of course, she didn't. Another thing that fascinated me was the fact that during a scene she walked as regally as a queen, but as soon as the cameras stopped rolling, she walked with a slouch. I often wondered whether that was because for such a tall lady she had such little feet.

She and I became very close during the whole production of this movie. As a matter of fact, she took great delight in introducing me to people as her daughter. Her comment was so realistic that about fifteen years ago I received a letter from a lady who had been a visitor on our set who wrote that she was always puzzled that whenever Miss Francis was interviewed in magazines she never mentioned that she had a daughter that was a famous child star!!

Kay was a very motherly and protective woman toward me and before I give you a small example of that, I'd like to digress for just a moment.

When shooting a movie, no matter what the climate, a soundstage is *never* air conditioned, or are there fans blowing or heaters going because those sounds would be picked up by the very sensitive microphones. In those days our lights were many times hotter than the ones used nowadays and depending on what costumes you were wearing it could get very uncomfortable to say the least. When Shirley Temple and I were making the movie *The Blue Bird* and the scenes between our two characters were supposedly set in the dead of winter. My character was that of a sickly and crippled girl who was wrapped up in a woolen shawl and blankets. At that time California was going through a heat wave and because of the hot lights and our costumes it became quite necessary for the make-up man to mop Shirley's and my forehead and face just a few seconds before the cameras rolled.

A similar situation occurred while making *Stella Parish*.

One day when it was excruciatingly hot on the set Kay asked for someone to bring her some ice cubes. She had noticed that my bangs were very moist and my cheeks seemed to be a bit red so she very lovingly rubbed the ice cubes on the wrists of my hands and told me that that would help cool my body temperature down. Even though I didn't really feel much difference, I loved her deeply for caring so much. And she was a woman who cared deeply for many people. Especially ones who were clearly "the underdog."

One evening many years ago, my husband Tony and I had dinner with a friend of mine who dated back to when I was making *Little Big Shot*. He had been an extra on that movie and perhaps a hundred more before he became a Hollywood columnist. That evening he told us that he had worked on a Kay Francis movie in which there had been a "rain" sequence where ultimately she and a group of extras were soaked to the skin. When the scene was over the wardrobe mistress handed Kay a towel and a blanket and placed her in front of a portable heater until the next scene was to be shot. For a split second Kay reached for the towel, but quickly withdrew her hands. Pointing to the extras she asked, "Do they get a blanket, a towel and a heater?" When the wardrobe lady shook her head no, Kay told her that until everyone received relief from the discomfort of the damp and cold Miss Francis wouldn't either.

That's why I personally got upset a number of years ago when I read a book entitled *Ginger, Loretta and Irene Who?* Although Miss Francis was not named in the title of the book there was a section that covered a period in her working life. The content absolutely denigrated her. To be very fair about the whole thing, I grant you that perhaps the author knew things about Kay that, as a child, I would not have known but he made the mistake of citing what happened on the sets of two of her movies. The only trouble was he chose the wrong two movies because they were *I Found Stella Parish* and *Comet Over Broadway*!!

Portraying her daughter in both of those movies I was on the set almost from beginning to the end so it was hard for me to believe what I was reading in that particular section of his book. There wasn't a true word in it!!

George Eells told of Kay Francis being so drunk that she held up production for over two weeks and that she could never remember her lines when she *was* able to turn up for work. Believe me, when working physically close to other actors you are *very* aware of their breath, for good or for bad. I am not saying that she did not drink…only that I never smelled any liquor on her breath and I have a very sensitive nose. Second of all, we were never held up for two weeks for *any* reason and I can guarantee you that Miss Francis was every bit of a professional lady and always knew her lines.

I think I made it clear in my autobiography that one of my pet peeves are authors that make up apocryphal tales about people that in many cases they have never even met. The danger in this is that they are usually very good writers and come across with such expertise that the reader is apt to believe their every word. I am grateful that there are such authors such as Scott O'Brien and the duo authors of Lynn Kear and John Rossman who took the time and patience when they did their own respective biographies on Kay to do a thorough job of research on her. To me, it is so unfair that many of the icons of the screen who are no longer living cannot defend themselves against authors who really don't care what impression they are leaving or how it hurts the loved ones who remain to face the blots made on the lives of their relative, lover or close friend. As long as it is within my power, and I am *reasonably* sure of my facts because "I was there," I will defend these great entertainers till my last breath. I hope someone will do the same for me one day.

When author Scott O'Brien was doing his revised and expanded edition of *I Can't Wait to Be Forgotten*, he asked if he could include my comments about the closeness that Kay and I shared. I hope that it helped a little bit when I wrote the following:

"We had such a wonderful connection that every scene that we did together came as easily and naturally as though we were interacting as mother and daughter in real life. Our director, Mervyn LeRoy, being the sensitive man that he was must have felt those vibes because, for the most part, he gave us the freedom of our natural compatibility with little direction coming from him. What a very wise and generous man he was to do this and it certainly paid off in the reviews because the critics picked up on that close mother and daughter connection without exception."

As I have mentioned before, in 1935 Kay Francis was Warners top box office champion and although she was not the type of person to ask for special privileges, the studio willingly gave her the largest and most luxurious dressing room-trailer of anyone on the lot. In addition to the trailer, she was handed the keys to one of the very few dressing rooms that were quartered in a separate building located away from the soundstages but on studio property.

These dressing rooms would be best described as fully furnished one-bedroom apartments with living room and kitchen facilities. Although this may seem excessive considering that the trailer provided more than enough comfort for the star in their working hours, there were a number of legitimate reasons that it proved advantageous to both the studio and their stars. It would not be an exaggeration to say that a lead in a motion picture is seen on the screen 75% of the time and the women stars have a particularly rougher schedule than the man has. To be ready on the set by 9:00 a.m. a woman's day starts in the make-up room at 6:00 a.m. She has to have her hair washed, dried and set and then make-up meticulously applied before she even gets into her costume. Naturally, the time extends if the make-up has to portray old age or sickness.

However, that early morning schedule does not end there. Unlike child stars, the adults often work well into the night and *still* have to be on the set ready to go by 9:00 a.m. the next morning. It stands to reason that going back to their homes only to sleep for one or two hours before having to return to the studio does not make any sense and the cameras would pick up that strain in their faces. The dressing room solves that problem. Many people think that spending the night on a dark movie studio lot would be very frightening. Not so. There were studio police patrolling the grounds all night long.

For just a moment I would like to intersperse a little humor while we are on the subject of dressing rooms.

It was an inside joke that the studio gave one of these very desirable dressing rooms to the studio's in-house bad boy, Errol Flynn. It was no secret that the handsome rascal used Hollywood as his playground and personally closed up every known and unknown bar every night.

The studio used to spend unknown hours in the mornings when he was due on the set trying to find him at his usual haunts or if his girlfriend of the moment or his wife would lock him out of the house. This way, with a dressing room, Flynn would head like a homing pigeon for this sanctuary and although somewhat worse for wear, the studio knew where to find him…most of the time.

I have brought up the fact of the luxuries Warners gave Kay Francis for a reason. In 1938 the studio was doing a bit of house cleaning and a lot of people were shaking in their boots wondering whether they would be next to get a pink slip. This included a lot of stars. However, the studio would use subtle ways in terminating the services of their once valued personalities.

In the case of Kay Francis the movies they offered her were not anywhere near the caliber they were in the past. Uncomplainingly, she accepted everything that was handed to her. In regards to myself I had not been given an assignment in three months and that was not a good sign. Anita and I were not surprised when my contract was not renewed, but before that happened I *was* given a part in a Kay Francis movie and once again I was going to portray her daughter. Another little girl had originally been assigned to that part. Although she was in a precarious situation herself, when Kay heard about it she said that if I wasn't going to play her daughter no one else would either.

I think the most horrendous thing that happened to this wonderful actress is that she was asked to remove her things from both her trailer and her dressing room because it was going to be given to another lady on the lot whose star was rising at a rapid pace. Bette Davis was replacing Kay Francis as Warners new hope and was inheriting all of the amenities that went with the position. Being the classy lady that she was Miss Francis offered no protests.

Kay stayed on to make a few movies after we did *Comet Over Broadway*, but by then she too left the studio along with such stalwart actors like Pat O'Brien. I was most fortunate to get a movie almost immediately called *Woman Doctor* and in the middle of production was offered a contract from two studios once my new movie was completed. My agent made his decision and I was eventually signed to Twentieth Century Fox. To find out what happened during my term at that studio I would suggest you read *My Fifteen Minutes*, as it also explains how it led to my career coming to an abrupt end.

I will never forget that most compassionate and loving actress, Miss Kay Francis. She may have had issues in her private life, but, as far as I am concerned, she was a person who gave much more than she ever received.

A Potpourri of Talent 45

With Jane Wyman in *Little Pioneer*.

Jane Wyman and I honored by Warner Bros. years later.

Cover of *Flickers* magazine (England).

A Potpourri of Talent   47

Dickie Moore and I in 1935.

And here we are in 2000.

Me as a paper doll!

Rudy Vallee and myself. Me with his picture 1935, and both of us at Warners when Jane Wyman and myself were honored.

Fans from Britain, Val and Stan Ball, present me with this mind-boggling 23, 000 cross-stitch reproduction of Al Jolson and myself. Picture here are (left to right) Val, me, Stan, and my daughter Toni.

Me, my uncle, and Anita taken on the grounds of Walter Lang's vacation home in Big Bear.

At a book signing in May 2007, with Jerry Lewis' son. Anthony.

A Potpourri of Talent 51

Me and Davey Lee. Davey was in *Sonny Boy* with Al Jolson.

Tony and I in our favorite place, Carmel, California.

With Turner Classic Movies' Bob Osborne.

I taught jr. drama at Famous Masguers Club. On the night of one of my productions with the kids, one of them couldn't turn up due to illness, so I grabbed her costume and replaced her. That's me in white. pointing.

At the Motion Picture Academy in 1986. With Darrel Hickman, Marcia Mae Jones, and Jerome Cortland.

With Allen Jones. A few years later. Allen sang one of my songs that I composed for my musical, *Garage Sale*.

A Potpourri of Talent   53

TALL, DARK, and CHARMING

It was mid-1938 when I was signed to a contract with Twentieth Century-Fox after my wonderful years at Warners came to an end. It was like leaving a very loving home but unfortunately at that time Warners felt it necessary to do some house cleaning and many of its valued family of actors were let go. It was an economical move but no matter what the reason the parting was sad for most of us.

However, it came as a pleasant surprise that my first part at Fox would be one in a movie starring Shirley Temple and this was exciting for a number of reasons. As I have explained before, I had never seen a Shirley Temple movie before and this was due to Jack Warner's dictum that I not be exposed to Shirley's mannerisms so that I would keep my uniqueness and not copy the princess of all child stars' mannerisms. Of course, I had seen her picture on the front of movie magazines and thought that she was the most beautiful child I had ever seen. And, of course, I also knew how famous and popular she was so I felt incredibly lucky that I was now going to be in the same movie as she was. That movie was *The Little Princess*.

Unlike at Warner Bros., I did not know any of the people behind the scenes like the cameraman, the assistant director and, of course, the cast. However, there are exceptions to every rule. Ian Hunter, who played Shirley's father in the movie, was my fellow Capetonian and we had worked together at Warners in two movies, *I Found Stella Parish* and *Comet Over Broadway*. Incongruously, we didn't have one scene together in *The Little Princess,* so a reunion was difficult seeing that when he worked I didn't and when I did, he didn't. Although the lovely Anita Louise and I had never worked together at Warners, where we were both under contract, we did see each other at previews and charity events and initially made contact that way. My sister Anita and the actress bonded together throughout the *Princess* movie, but a number of years later, because we both knew Anita Louise as the loving and gentle soul that she was, we were very saddened to hear that in her later life she had a problem with alcohol and died much too young.

Hollywood, in the thirties and forties, had a huge British colony. Its members regularly gathered to celebrate British holidays and most belonged to various clubs like the famous cricket club started by that famous character actor Sir Aubrey Smith. Needless to say, Anita and I had met Arthur Treacher at these various functions and enjoyed his sense of humor immensely. As a matter of fact, he had the cast of *Princess* in stitches with his dry sense of humor, which made coming to work a joy!!!

When it came to Richard Greene, who played the romantic lead to Anita Louise, all the females, young and old alike, agreed that he was much too beautiful to be a man. I must say, that to his credit, he always played that fact down, which in itself was very unusual in Hollywood. Many years later, at a Jeanette Mac Donald banquet, several of us guest stars were seated at the dais and as the evening progressed, the lovely woman seated next to me mentioned how impressed she had been with the acting job I had done as Becky, the little cockney girl in *The Little Princess*. In the process of talking about the various actors on that movie Richard Greene's name came up. None of us had been called up to the podium as yet so this lady and I had not been introduced. She looked very familiar to me, but one must remember that when we get to the point of being guest stars at nostalgia banquets we have all "aged" somewhat and some of us do not look like we used to.

The "Becky" doll. taken at Warner Bros. with the manufacturer of the doll.

To my wonderment, she spoke glowingly about Richard Greene and mentioned she had never known a finer man. It was at this point that the hostess of the evening started introducing us so therefore all private conversations came to an end. It was only when this lovely actress was introduced that I realized how wonderful and unusual her statements were about Richard Greene. Her name was Patricia Medina, who had been married to Richard but they had divorced and she was, at that time, Mrs. Joseph Cotten. I think the biggest compliment anyone can give another person is an ex-spouse being complimentary about the other and there was no doubt she sincerely meant everything that she had said about him.

Tall, Dark and Charming is the title of this chapter and it is my description of Cesar Romero. It was never a false attitude on his part and females sensed this honesty in him. Every leading lady in Hollywood wanted him as her escort to movie previews and especially social events because Butch (as all of his friends called him) was an incredibly gifted dancer. He and I had few scenes together but we socialized on the set much more so than Ian Hunter and I did. There were many young girl actresses in this movie and Cesar took the time to joke with them and you could see the color in their cheeks rising as they appreciated his attention. He had a very warm heart and had no difficulty showing it to one and all.

When I first met my husband-to-be, Anthony Drake, he had never seen *The Little Princess* and when we visited Walter and Fieldsie Lang at their home I had mentioned it. Before one could blink an eye, Walter said he would arrange for a showing of it at Fox and he would get in touch with us when a definite date had been set. True to his word, about ten days later, Walter had procured a projection room for us and we were to meet in front of that building at Fox.

The day came and we all met outside the projection room and I was delighted that Cesar Romero had joined us because he hadn't seen the movie in a long time. As we stood there waiting for the projection room to open up, I saw, off in the distance, a small figure of a man smoking a huge cigar. It was Mr. Darryl F. Zanuck, my reluctant boss from the past. (You might want to read *My Fifteen Minutes* to understand why I called him my reluctant boss.) That day he never approached any of us, but from the look that he gave me I saw that nothing had changed. I still represented an inconvenience to him. Yet, history will tell you that I wasn't the first or last person to get that kind of treatment from the man that headed Twentieth Century-Fox Studios.

Walter Lang's Big Bear vacation home.

I am happy to say that that certainly did not put a damper on a day that turned out to be a lot of fun and quite a nice experience for Tony. We laughed so much in the projection viewing room because the showing was essentially for Tony and they had edited the movie down mainly to feature all the scenes I was in. Good naturedly, Cesar started grumbling that what remained of his part, which was small to start with, would make him eligible to be a member of the Screen Extras Guild. Needless to say that, thanks to Walter, a good time was had by all and Tony got to see his best girl doing her "stuff" as a little cockney maid!!

Before that showing and even before I met Tony, I had been invited to a special event held by the Motion Picture Mothers Club. This was a yearly event and the main theme of the party was that the mothers of celebrities would bring their famous offspring and introduce them at the beginning of the evening. It was a charitable organization and for those who were not members of this exclusive club paid a rather steep price for a ticket to attend. All monies collected that night went to a specified charitable organization. To start off the evening and before the dinner and dance started the mothers, one by one, stood up and introduced their famous offspring. I happened to be seated at the table with Cesar, his mother, and his date for the evening, the lovely and talented actress Andrea Leeds. It was amazing how much Cesar looked like his mother. She was approximately his height, had the same color and type of hair that he had and was just as charming and had the same warm personality of that of her son.

Imagine my surprise when after she had risen and introduced her boy to the audience she said she had one more introduction to make. She announced that seeing that "this dear little actress did not have family to represent her," she was stepping in to temporarily act as her "mother." Mrs. Romero graciously told me to stand up and she said, "And here is my daughter for the evening, Sybil Jason." I had a hard time keeping the tears back at her beautiful gesture.

After all of the introductions had been made by the motion picture mothers, and as the tradition decreed, the first dance was between mother and son or father and daughter. It was so un-Hollywood-like and so beautiful to watch and observe the great love and respect each one had for the other. After that first dance was over Cesar escorted his mother back to the table and bent to whisper something into Andrea Leeds' ear. She gave him a warm smile and squeezed his hand affectionately and it was then that Cesar took my hand and led me onto the dance floor. We must have been a sight to see because I am exceptionally short and my dear friend and co-worker was exceptionally tall but he was such a wonderful dancer that we glided very easily across the floor. I have since made a joke that all of my dancing partners happened to have always been tall and for that reason I have viewed the handsomest belt buckles in town!!

With Joan Leslie.

The next time that I saw Cesar was years later, long after the Fox viewing of *The Little Princess*. It was a special birthday party held for Bette Davis and I happened to be seated on the dais with other Warner Bros. alumni. Cesar was seated at one of the premier tables reserved for special celebrities.

After the party was over Joan Leslie, Jeffrey Lynn, Ernest Borgnine, Cesar and I met for some talk and drinks and I have got to tell you that Cesar looked more handsome that night than any other time I had ever seen him. His hair was snow white, his skin was tan and smooth and he had a gorgeous white beard. He was breathtaking.

I did not see Cesar for years after that night. The next time was at an historic nostalgia evening held by the American Cinema Awards. Robert Wagner was the master of ceremonies and he had the job of introducing 300 of us one at a time and allowing us to bow and get our kudos from the audience. What an exciting evening that was. Every star that was still alive attended and we were all entertained by the likes and talents of Liza Minnelli, Cab Calloway, and Vanessa Williams. At the end of the evening, as we were all leaving the banquet room, Cesar and I bumped into each other and as usual it was a joy to see him again. Unfortunately, he did not look well, but I thought that he might have been going through the rigors of the flu bug that was going around at that time of year. We did not see each other again, but, as usual, we exchanged Christmas cards and warm messages at the end of 1993. I was watching the news on television on New Year's Day, January 1, 1994 and there was an interruption for a news flash. Cesar Romero had died on the first day of that New Year. The world may have lost a very popular actor, but I lost a very dear friend.

BORN TO DANCE

I find it so hard to believe that even now with the public's awareness of just about everything concerning Hollywood stars that the majority of people that I meet or receive letters from are under the impression that we all know each other.

Nothing could be further from the truth. Of course, when you make a lot of movies and attend many show business functions you are bound to meet a lot of the prominent stars, but that is not what I am talking about. You have never seen a more thrilled person than a major star meeting another one whom they have always admired but had never met before. Because they are actors, you wouldn't see them jumping up and down with excitement, but I assure you they certainly feel it. The most amusing thing to see is for one star to ask another for their autograph. Yes, that *really* does happen. I have seen that a number of times and have done it myself. But perhaps using the word amusing has the wrong connotation in describing such an event. I can only speak for myself and for some stars who have agreed that they felt the same way I did, that no matter how self confident one is in their profession it all goes out of the window when it comes to asking for the autograph of someone you admire. Inwardly, you become very sheepish and hope that you are not infringing upon their privacy or worse yet that they think you are some kind of an idiot.

It has always been a wonderful experience for me because just about everyone had been more than gracious and in some instances a star has become a very valued friend. If you look at one or two of my pressbooks, you will see press clippings where I am appearing in person at a theater and a movie starring a prominent star is showing on that same bill. This is repeated many times when I used to do personal appearances across the country and into Canada.

Sometimes I was allowed to sit in the backseat of a theater after I have made my appearance and watch the movie. Nobody in the audience ever discovered me sitting there after they had seen me on stage because the thought never occurred to them that I would do such a thing. It never failed that when an Eleanor Powell movie was playing I would want to see it. I guess it was because my career had started on stage as a dancer and I realized how hard her routines were and what a fantastic tap dancer she really was!! Getting back to my pressbooks, it was quite strange to see us side by side in theater ads and also in articles featuring "up-and-coming stars" and the fact that we had never met. That held true until I was an adult.

After I had voluntarily decided not to continue my career as an actress in the early '50s, I was still being invited to be a guest star at many of the nostalgic banquets honoring those of us of the Golden Era. You really never know who your fellow honorees are going to be until you get to the hotel or wherever the banquet is being held, so you can imagine my surprise and thrill as I was escorted up to the dais and seated right next to me was…ELEANOR POWELL!! In my mind's eye my jaw dropped to my ankles, but I had sufficient control to just tell her how much of a pleasure it was to meet her at long last.

3 pictures at Eleanor Powell's birthday.
Upper left: With famous writer. Adela Rogers St. John.
Upper right: Me and Ellie Being honored at a banquet.
Lower: Me getting my birthday cake too (Virginia O'Brien in background).

Eleanor Powell was *everything* that one would wish a star to be. She was quite a beautiful lady and did not look her age at that time and better yet she had a warm and giving personality and adored a good laugh. And Ellie laughed a lot! (Have you noticed that most of the Golden Era ladies had a good sense of humor?)

If one believed in reincarnation one would swear that from the word go Ellie and I had had a close relationship in another time and another age. We bonded almost immediately and right after that evening we made arrangements to get together on a strictly social/personal level. However, before that happened, I received word from a theater owner who was going to give Ellie a special surprise birthday party on November 21, held at his theater in Hollywood. He wanted me to be one of the special guests. Naturally, I didn't mention this to her because it was going to be a surprise party!

What an evening that was!! The audience was packed to the rafters with people that Ellie had worked with at MGM and also many of her personal friends. Ellie was seated on the stage and a blindfold was put on her so that when they joined her on stage and talked to her she would have to guess who was there to honor her. Ellie had a really good ear and guessed who most of her guests were. However, when it came to my turn to speak to her, I decided to use my cockney "Becky" accent and see if I could fool her. I did!

She admitted that it drove her crazy that she couldn't identify one of her friends but when the blindfold came off she gave me a huge bear hug and said I was a little pixie for fooling her!! After all the surprise appearances had been made, a big table was rolled onto the stage and one huge birthday cake was on it and also a smaller one was beside it. Imagine my surprise when it was announced that I was to return to the stage and blow out the candles of the smaller cake as November 23 was *my* birthday. After that wonderful night Ellie and I made arrangements to get together socially and not wait till the next nostalgia banquet.

Most of our get-togethers centered around one of our homes. Tony and I had a home in Studio City and in our backyard we had converted a three-car garage into a private little theatre. We did it all ourselves and it became a favorite gathering place for our friends. Tony had constructed a projection booth and papered it with Laurel and Hardy black-and-white wallpaper. He had also built a proscenium on our small stage and cast some beautiful angels which he painted gold around it. I made bright red velvet curtains that could be controlled either backstage or in the projection booth and we even had a very small dressing room backstage. Our "theater seats" were real Barnum and Bailey folding chairs that Tony shellacked to a high gloss and when we weren't using the stage we had a pretty big screen that Tony would project a lot of our friends' movies on. Some times we were incredibly lucky when one of our producer friends would lend us a 16mm print of their movie that had not even been released as yet. We had some marvelous evenings there and, as I mentioned in my first book, my dear friend Peggy Ann Garner fell so much in love with our little theater she wanted to move into it!!

When I started this chapter, the main thought that kept swirling around in my head was "What would the fans of Eleanor Powell really like the most to know about her?" I am presuming that it would be anything that is not on public record. In other words, anything that describes what the woman, *not* the actress, was really like." Luckily, I can do that because I was very fortunate to have had her as one of my dearest friends.

Ellie was one of the most down-to-earth people I have ever met in my life. She radiated warmth and a personal charm that came very easily to a person who did not have to dig down deep to come up with this persona. This *was* Eleanor Powell.

When I met Ellie she had been divorced from her husband, Glenn Ford, for a number of years and had started a brand-new chapter in her life. She had given up her large home and opted for a simpler standard of living by becoming an apartment dweller. Her apartment was right across the street from Roxbury Park in Beverly Hills, where I occasionally played tennis as a child, and because she lived on a second-floor level she had a great view of the park and its landscape.

Eleanor had many interests and one of them was her religious beliefs. She was a member of the Unity Church. She worked closely with children, teaching them at Sunday school, which led to a TV series called *Faith of Our Children*, which won Ellie five local Emmy Awards.

Glenn Ford and self as judges at a beauty contest.

In the interim, she made a very good friend who became her closest companion and secretary, Eleanor Debus. Two more compatible people you would never meet and she became very important to the peace of mind of Eleanor Powell. One of the things that Ellie made a priority in her life was that all fan mail letters were promptly seen to and responded to. This was made doubly important because as the years went by the mail became overwhelming, especially after the release of MGM's *That's Entertainment!* Eleanor Debus kept all phases of Ms. P's business life in balance and, amongst other things, made it possible that no fan letter was ever overlooked or not answered.

I think one of the most amusing Eleanor Powell stories I have ever heard came from Ellie herself. Tony and I were spending a very casual evening with Ellie at her apartment and somehow the conversation turned to recipes. I had just gotten through telling her about the good Indian curry that I make and she said one of the most successful dinners she ever made was a comparatively simple one.

As I previously said, Ellie's apartment was on the second floor of her building. Because she was such an early riser, she would check to see if the paper boy had thrown her downstairs neighbor' paper in a reachable spot and if not she would retrieve it and place it in front of her neighbor's front door.

One morning she bumped into her neighbor and was surprised to see her up that early and to see that she was visibly upset. It seems that she was expecting guests for dinner that night and was going to cook a roast for them.

This was something she had never attempted to do before this night and she had planned to prepare it early enough in the early afternoon so that she wouldn't be rushed. She had a phone call from her pregnant daughter, who lived in Santa Barbara, at 5:00 a.m. that morning saying that she didn't feel too well and wanted to see her doctor, whose offices were in Beverly Hills. Of course, her priority was going to pick up her daughter and drive her back to Beverly Hills, but she didn't have any phone number to get in touch with her dinner guests to cancel out the dinner.

Ellie just squeezed her hand and told her to go get her daughter, give her the key to her apartment and Ellie would cook the roast for her. The woman couldn't believe what she was hearing but she was told not to waste time on words and just to get going on her journey to Santa Barbara.

The neighbor was able to drive her daughter to the doctor, where, much to their relief, there was nothing seriously wrong with her daughter. With that in mind, they scurried back to her apartment because her guests were due at her place in fifteen minutes time. As they entered the apartment, they saw Ellie putting the finishing touches of flowers on the table she had set so beautifully and informed them, cool as a cucumber, that the dinner was ready and that the roast came out especially nicely. Before the guests were to arrive momentarily, Ellie was about to leave the two stunned women when they begged her to join all of them for dinner. Ellie just smiled and thanked them, but she said she had some chores to accomplish that night but wished them all a lovely evening anyway.

I can only imagine the faces of Ellie's neighbor's guests when she told them that the whole dinner was prepared for them by none other than Eleanor Powell!! I wonder if they thought that maybe their hostess had imbibed a little too much wine before dinner!! Ellie was always so generous toward all of her friends.

There wasn't a wedding anniversary that Tony and I celebrated that we didn't receive flowers and a beautiful gift from her. As I had told you previously, our birthdays were so close in days that quite a few times Ellie and I made it a mutual birthday celebration. However, on one particular birthday, I wanted to give my dear friend something really special that she would like, but I just couldn't seem to come up with any great or unusual idea. May I tell you that my husband was an exceptionally fine artist and had been doing a series of oil paintings that he called *The Chair* paintings. What he did was paint a director's chair with the subject's name imprinted in block letters on the flap of the chair. Then, on the seat of the chair, he painted something very dear or significant in their lives and on the floor beside the chair a sample of something that described their career. In some cases it could be reversed. As an example, he had just done one for Bob Hope and on the chair was a golf ball and a golf club and on the floor were some of his famous movie scripts.

Tony suggested that if I liked the idea he would do one for Ellie. I was completely thrilled by the idea and I just knew Ellie would be too.

One evening the intercom came on (Tony was painting in our little theater in our backyard) and he said he had just finished her painting and would I like to see it. I don't think I ever turned off the intercom, but made a beeline toward the "theater." It was a beautiful painting, but peripherally I saw Tony shaking his head. I asked him what was wrong. He said the tap shoes weren't right. The one shoe was heel and sole down and the other was placed on its side with the taps showing. They looked fine to me. You see, Tony had used my little tap shoes as a model for Ellie's tap shoes to paint on the seat of the chair and to my horror he took some neutral paint and blanked the shoes out!! I thought he had gone mad!! He said to just give him time and he would replace a better version of the shoes. In fact, he was also very unhappy with the red rose that he had placed next to the shoes.

A few days later he called me in to see the "new and improved" painting. The shoes were definitely different and the rose had turned into a yellow one instead of a red one. No matter what, it was a great painting and I couldn't wait for the evening when we would take it over to our dear friend.

Let me give you a visual. My husband was a six-foot, slim, but well-muscled man, but when Ellie opened up the gift she lifted my husband up in a bear hug as if he weighed a mere basketful of feathers!! She loved the painting and when I explained all of the changes he had made she left us for a minute and came out with her tap shoes. It seems she had these made up especially for her and when Fred Astaire and Gene Kelly had admired them they went to her shoemaker and had the same shoes made for them. They couldn't use them as the configuration of the taps was just too different and way too slippery for their needs.

She was stunned and so were all of us, including the artist himself, that the shoes Tony had painted were just like the ones she now held in her hands. They were completely different from the old-fashioned style of my tap shoes. To put a cherry on top of this story is that her favorite color rose was…yellow!!

When Eleanor Powell passed away she didn't forget her friends. Personally, she left me some beautiful things that I treasure to this day, but what I hold most dear are the memories I have of a very special lady and a great star. One can never replace a true blue friend and I miss her to this very day, but I am very grateful we shared some wonderful times together.

When Silence Was Truly Golden

Before the Warner Brothers and Al Jolson changed the history of Hollywood in 1927 by producing the first talkie, *The Jazz Singer*, the world had been entertained by the antics of such stars as Mary Pickford, Charlie Chaplin, Buster Keaton, Harold Lloyd, Fatty Arbuckle, the Gish sisters, and so many others too numerous to mention. They starred in literally hundreds of silent movies which could be enjoyed worldwide because there was no need to understand the English language to be entertained by what was going on on the screen. This certainly was a boon to our newly arrived immigrants to America.

The silent era was not only comedy, but it had its sexy idols too in the magnificent forms of Rudolph Valentino, Douglas Fairbanks, Sr., and not forgetting the *femme fatale* leading ladies like Theda Bara. I do not know whether it was an apocryphal tale, but I have heard that Theda Bara took her name from the anagram of "Arab Death"!!

I know I have left out the names of so many silent screen stars and for that I hope I will be forgiven, but I'm sure there must be an author who has taken the gauntlet and produced a fascinating book on the silent era and its stars at some time or other. I do not have the expertise to write with authority about that era and shall not even attempt to do so, but from the little experience I had with meeting some of the greats of this era I can certainly say that they were a fascinating and as diverse a group of people one could ever hope to meet.

It never fails to amaze me to notice the excitement an author feels when they are interviewing an icon from the Golden Era of Hollywood. I certainly can relate to that because it was exactly how I felt when I had the privilege of meeting some of the greatest icons of the silent movie era and, in some cases, the early vaudevillians. Previously I touched lightly on vari-

66 Five Minutes More

Tie-ins with Marion Davies, Bette Davis, Kay Francis, Errol Flynn and Dick Powell.

ous stars of the silent screen era like Marion Davies and Mary Pickford, but it was mainly after they had retired from acting or were primarily known for sound movies, like the madcap comedies of Carole Lombard.

A TRUE GENIUS

My very first experience with an icon from the silent era came one day when my guardians and I were preparing to go to a party in Beverly Hills. It was going to be an informal affair, but I could tell by the vibes of my sister and uncle that this was going to be a very special party due to the preparations they were going through before we left for the party.

When we got there, we noticed that the event was being held on the tennis court of the enormous estate of the owner and star that lived there. Of course, I knew what our host looked like. Everyone in the world did. But as I perused all of the famous faces who were filling their plates with wonderful food set out to please any palette, there was no one that I saw that vaguely resembled our host. When my sister Anita and my uncle Harry and I joined everyone on the tennis court, a very nice gentleman approached us and welcomed us to his home. I was a bit puzzled why this gentleman was saying that this was his home because he looked nothing like what I was expecting to see. This man had wild-looking, wiry, grey hair, was on the short side and had a decided cockney accent! However, it didn't take me too long to realize that this gentleman was indeed Charlie Chaplin because of the great attention everyone was paying to him and how he graciously was making sure that everyone had what they needed in food and drink. He was dressed in tennis whites, as were most of his men guests, and from the conversation that I overheard, it seems he was an excellent tennis player.

I never saw Mr. Chaplin sit down the whole afternoon we spent there. He just darted back and forth and made conversation with everyone that was there and left no one out. Including me. When he approached Anita and my uncle and me he asked if we were enjoying being in America and had we met most of the British colony of actors yet. He seemed truly interested in our responses.

When it came to me, he said he had a question to ask me. He said that he enjoyed my first movie very much and especially liked the imitations I had done in *Little Big Shot* and was it true I had done the same imitations on the stages of South Africa and London? I thanked him for his compliments and said it was perfectly true that I had done those imitations on stage and even more of them that weren't in the movie. He wanted a rundown of all the imitations that I had done in the past. When I got through naming them, he asked me *the* question. "How is it you never imitated me?" I was shocked when he asked me that and it took me a while before I could stammer out, "Be…Because Charlie Chaplin…didn't talk!!" He just burst out laughing and said, "Very good, my dear. Very good!" He was a marvelous host and I felt very comfortable with him because he seemed to know just what to say to everyone.

Bordering on early evening the tennis court was cleared and the lights lit up the court like it was daylight. It was time for the adults to play a few games of tennis and we watched for a while, but common sense told us that it was time that a young child should make herself scarce because this was "adult time." Being ever alert, Mr. Chaplin saw us ready to depart and came over to us to thank us for coming to his party and that he hoped that we would all meet again in the near future. We *did* meet again not long after that afternoon.

I was scheduled to head the entertainment part of the British Ball that the Consulate held at the Biltmore Hotel ballroom which would benefit needy Brits. Warners loaned us the Busby Berkeley girls so that we could recreate our dance from my Technicolor short *The Changing of the Guard* and the headlines in the newspapers a few days before the event said that the first people to buy tickets for it were Charlie Chaplin and Paulette Goddard. Naturally, the rest of the Brits of Hollywood followed suit and the Consulate put the money realized to good use. I was very proud of the fact that Miss Goddard and Mr. Chaplin gave me and the girls a standing ovation for our dance.

The next time that I saw Mr. Chaplin and Paulette was when we shared a box at the Sonja Henie Ice Capades. A lot of pictures were taken of the three of us and they must be in the archives of either *The Los Angeles Times* or *Herald Examiner*, but, unfortunately, I do not have any myself. I was there specifically that night to present Miss Henie with a huge bouquet of flowers. After her last skating presentation a pathway of wood planks were put down on the ice so that I could walk up to her and give her the flowers. That was a thrilling experience for me because I have always been a devotee of ice skating. To me it's like ballet on ice and in my adult years my dear husband was so very patient with me when the ice-skating shows came on television because he would join me and watch for hours of what I considered superb artistry on ice without complaint. While Mr. Chaplin and Paulette and I shared our box seats just off the ice, they both were very much enthralled by Miss Henie and her company of ice skaters and clapped as heartily as any of the audience that attending the show that evening. Mr. Chaplin had a lot of his little movie character in him, for it came very easily for him to appreciate what he was seeing by displaying an abundance of childlike enthusiasm. It is true he may have been a genius to the world, but he was as much fun as if he truly was that adorable Little Tramp each time that I met him.

DAREDEVIL COMEDIAN

The first time I was introduced to Harold Lloyd was a day when I attended the Barnum and Bailey Circus. It is a fact of movie life that even when one is attending a child -loving event like the circus, even that becomes a photo opportunity for the press.

Anita and my uncle and I were enthralled with what was going on in the three rings of the circus and although every now and again we were distracted by a camera flash going off near us as people or the press were taking pictures of us, we really weren't disturbed by it. In a strange sort of way one becomes used to these distractions and after a while accepts it as just part of one's job. However, the expanded version of this was not that comfortable, especially for a child who is enjoying her very first time at the circus.

Several press people came directly over to us and asked my guardians whether they could take me over to Harold Lloyd and his children so that our pictures could be taken together for their story that would be in the next day's paper.

Regrettably but acquiescing to their request, Anita and I followed the reporters over to where Harold and the kids were. Mr. Lloyd was very nice and it was obvious that he liked children because he mentioned that he was sorry that my time had been interrupted by the press on such a fun occasion. Our pictures were taken, and, satisfied that they had obtained what they wanted, the reporters left and Anita and I had a few moments with Mr. Lloyd, Gloria Lloyd, Harold, Jr. and their adopted daughter, Peggy. The conversation was mostly with Harold because the kids were engrossed in watching the trapeze artists getting ready to put on their most breathtaking act. But before we left Mr. Lloyd insisted that we take his phone number and address and wanted ours in return so that he could invite me up to play with the kids sometime. It was very nice meeting all of them, but I couldn't wait to get back to our seats so that I too could watch the trapeze artists.

With Harold Lloyd.

I wasn't that lucky.

My uncle had made arrangements with some reporters for me to go back of the tent area and pose with some of the main attractions for their stories on the circus the next day. I never did see the trapeze act because after that, for some reason or other, we left to go home. I would guess that it was because the tent show was almost over and we could beat the crowd getting to our car. Rather sad but, let's face it, this too was "part of the job."

We didn't have to wait long for a phone call from Harold Lloyd. He said that his kids were looking forward to me spending the day with them and he asked what date would be convenient to do this. It was a very rare occasion that I was not working on a movie, but I was waiting for my next assignment, which had not come as yet, so I was free to go visit them for the afternoon. He assured Anita that I would be well supervised and safe at all times and believe me he didn't exaggerate one little bit. I have never been in such a large home in my life. The grounds themselves went on and on and as far as the kids were concerned they had everything right there to delight any child in the way of toys, games, you name it.

The Lloyd chauffeur called for me and when we got to their house my jaw dropped from the immensity of it all. You can imagine what I thought when I went into their living room that was huge to start with and saw a Christmas tree that stretched up to their ceiling and believe me their ceiling was high. I was told that the Christmas tree stayed there all year long. In today's vernacular I thought that was pretty cool!!

The kids and I had a great lunch and then we were allowed to go play on the grounds, *but* there were restrictions.

Because the grounds were so vast and the Lloyds wanted their kids and their guests to be safe at all times we weren't allowed to wander away to another site. That was hardly a restriction because the play area that was okayed for us was huge! Later, I heard that their home was called Greenacres and it was definitely a family-oriented home, even though it was known as one of the show places of early Hollywood. Very generously, Mr. and Mrs. Lloyd would often allow events to take place on their grounds held by various organizations that would use the funds realized at these affairs to benefit needy recipients of that organization.

The day that I spent at the Lloyds home was most enjoyable and although when late afternoon approached and I was invited to dinner I wasn't able to accept because I had to do a radio broadcast that evening. I was invited back several times, but in the years 1935 through 1937 I was a very busy little girl and had little time to spare. I would have loved to spend more time with the Lloyd kids because they all were very nice, but time and circumstance would not allow for it.

May I say that Charlie Chaplin and Harold Lloyd were as different as day to night when it came to personalities. Their movie persona was that of comics and neo-tragediennes but that's where the similarity ended. As I had mentioned before, Mr. Chaplin had a lot of the Little Tramp in him for he had a child-like enthusiasm for many things and easily displayed his pleasure for them in that manner. Mr. Lloyd, on the other hand, was a real family man, rather quiet at times, and he too had a great enthusiasm for life in general, but it was not generated in a child-like way. It was obvious that Mrs. Lloyd and her husband had a good and stable marriage and delighted in all of their children.

And talking about their children, I did meet one of them once again at an event that Jackie Coogan and I were Master and Mistress of ceremonies many, many years later. It was like the Oscars, but only for juvenile actors and actresses of movies and television. The presenters were all ex-kid child stars handing the top prizes to the youngsters in the spotlight of the year 1979.

During a rehearsal break a young lady, who had very sad eyes, came up to me and said, "Hi, Sybil. Remember me?" I didn't know what to say and I didn't want to tell her that I didn't recognize her at all so I said, "How long has it been?" hoping to get a hint at who she was. It didn't help. She said, "A long, long time." There was an awkward pause and she finally said, "You *don't* remember me, do you," I felt my face getting really red with embarrassment. I finally had to admit that I didn't, but that if it was that we only knew each other as kids it was likely that we had changed in looks so much that it would be hard to recognize each other.

Bingo!! She agreed, although she didn't make it easy by saying that my face and eyes hadn't changed so much that she wouldn't have recognized me. While I gulped a bit she finally took me off the hook and said that she was Peggy Lloyd, the adopted daughter of Harold and Mildred Lloyd. I truly was happy to see her again and told her perhaps we could do catch up when we broke for rehearsal lunch. We did and Edith Fellows and Peggy Ann Garner joined us. She was not a happy woman, by any means, and I must admit she had reasons not to be. If I remember correctly she was extremely close to Harold. One would never guess that she was any different than his other kids the way he treated her. He doted on all of his kids and Peggy just idolized her father.

The next hour was a shocker as Peggy updated us. I only knew her as Peggy, but she told us that her full legal name was Marjorie Elisabeth Lloyd and she was adopted when she was a little one of five years old.

The little time that I spent with the Lloyds they all represented a very close and happy family. Apparently, when the kids were older that was not the case for Harold Jr. or Peggy. To put it delicately, Harold Jr. (or Duke as

Me and Edith Fellows at a benefit for a paraplegic child.

he was fondly nicknamed) was confused with his sexual identity and many times arrived back at his home beaten up. It seems he never tried to defend himself. His dad was very accepting of his son, but apparently his son was not accepting of himself. Although every thing written about Harold Jr. said he died of a massive stroke a few months after his father passed away, Peggy told us that Harold Jr. had committed suicide. I cannot verify this because I have not read this anywhere else. The only time I ever heard this was from Peggy. Apparently, Peggy's adult years were not happy ones and the biggest shock of her life was when her adopted father died (her adopted mother died before him) and she learned that she was completely left out of the will. She said it was like she never existed. She told us that she never accepted this deletion because as far as she was concerned she was even closer to her father than Gloria was. I should point out that I am not stating all of these details as fact. I am only reporting what Peggy told us that day.

My heart went out to her and I cannot tell you where she is today, as that was the last time I ever saw her. I do hope that wherever she is she is a much happier woman and that she has made a better life for herself.

I NEVER CALLED HIM FATTY

In the mid-'70s, because I had done quite a bit of charity work for various Southern California organizations, one of our Los Angeles city council members, who had already awarded me a city plaque, had invited my husband Tony and myself as guests to a political event held at the famous Hollywood Palladium. As Tony and I walked to our table a lot of wonderful memories flooded my mind. In 1940 my sister Anita and I had been invited to the opening of the Palladium and what an exciting event that was! Every star imaginable attended and if memory serves me right I *think* the orchestra that night was Tommy Dorsey and his singers were Frank Sinatra and Connie Haines. Many years later, and because my husband loved to dance, we spent many a date night on the ballroom floor and rarely sat down at our table till almost closing time. Right across the street from the Palladium was a small but charming Italian restaurant that we never failed to visit after expending a goodly portion of energy on the dance floor throughout the evening.

However, that night, in the mid-'70s, when we attended the political event, it ushered in two significant happenings for me, both of which were totally unexpected. Through choice, when our daughter Toni was born, I decided to devote all of my time to being a full-time mother and I never regretted a single second of it. (For a more detailed explanation that led up to this evening at the Palladium I suggest you read *My Fifteen Minutes*.)

We were seated at a table with some very interesting people. Most of them were politically bent, but there was one man and one woman

My first meeting with Minta Arbuckle at the Palladium. with Los Angeles Police Chief Davis

who seemed to take special note as I was telling our table of my experiences with some of Hollywood's most famous icons. The gentleman happened to be a personal manager and the lady sitting next to him was Minta Durfee Arbuckle, who was Charlie Chaplin's first leading lady and the first wife of Fatty Arbuckle. I was absolutely thrilled to meet her and I wanted to ask her a million questions, but by this time the entertainment on the stage had stopped and the political business was first on the agenda.

Again with Minta, honored at an Evening of Stars.

As happens at most events when the business at hand was over it was time to take pictures with the guest stars of the politicos at the end of the evening. However, before that happened, the personal manager, Mr. William Thrush, gave me his card and asked if I would be interested in doing a lecture tour. Of course, that had never entered my mind, but he said that he and Mrs. Arbuckle were so impressed with the stories that I told, which seemed to captivate the people at our table, that he felt sure I could captivate an audience with these same stories. To read the progression of this idea I will not repeat myself as it is all in my other book, but I will say that I took Mr. Thrush up on his offer and in the interim enjoyed myself thoroughly doing it. The big bonus was getting to know Minta very well because she too was one of his clients.

On location with Minta for *Nectar of the Gods*, a semi-documentary about Northern California vineyards.

Bill Thrush kept both of us individually busy and when we were becoming old timers at this lecture game, one day he called a meeting with Minta and me. He had been approached by an independent producer up in Northern California to co-star Minta and me in a semi-documentary about the vineyards in that part of the country and it was going to be called *Nectar of the Gods*. They would incorporate the appearance of actors that represented the Keystone Kops and we actually had one of the originals doing a scene with both Minta and me. She was a perfect joy to work with and in between scenes she would

On the lecture tour.

enthrall me with personal stories of all the silent stars she had worked with or knew very well. To hear her banter around names like Rudolph Valentino, Theda Bara, Gloria Swanson, the Gish sisters, Mabel Normand, ad infinitum, was absolutely mind boggling. Months later, Minta followed my appearance at a theater in San Francisco with that of her own and I was so very fortunate to get her on audio tape talking about all of her fellow silent picture stars and her experiences with them. In private Minta went into detail about her marriage to her Roscoe. She said she *never* called him Fatty…only Roscoe. She adored him and he was definitely the love of her life, even though they eventually divorced after having been married for seventeen years. However, she never regretted marrying him as he had always been so generous to her and been a very loving husband. They regrettably separated in 1921 for various reasons and this was before they both suffered the horrendous scandal of the death of Virginia Rappe. During Arbuckles' lengthy three trials regarding his purported actions that led to the starlet's death, Minta stuck voraciously by his side and didn't divorce him until 1925. Fatty married again, but Minta never did. There was only one man in her life till the very day she died. Minta had a home in the Silverlake district. I'm sure when she first owned it was a lovely neighborhood, but many years had taken its toll but this was her home and that's where she was going to stay. We often shared afternoon tea together and I noticed that she was making rather odd friends that seemed to know their way around her house. It was none of my business so I didn't mention that I thought perhaps she should be a little more circumspect with opening up her home so generously to strangers, but she seemed comfortable with them. After all it must have been very lonely living in her home all by herself.

    I must tell you that Minta, as we short people can tell you, was pretty vain about appearing taller than she actually was and absolutely insisted on wearing spike heels. Mr. Thrush kept on warning her that at her age it would be so much safer to wear a lower heel and not chance taking a fall. Advanced age or not, Minta wanted to be glamorous for her public no matter what the circumstance and insisted on wearing her considerable wardrobe of spiked-heeled shoes. Unfortunately, that dear lady paid with her life for that bit of vanity. Even after she had taken a fall and then recuperated she was very anxious to look her best because there was a movie producer that was interested in doing a movie about Minta's life. Even though she knew I was not interested in returning to work on a regular movie (the semi-documentary that we had done had been okay by me) she insisted that I portray her in the story of her life. Before that got to any further meetings Minta took another terrible fall due to wearing her beloved spike heels and, unfortunately, that led to complications that ended her life. What saddened me was the fact that she had always been so very proud of the beautiful ring that Fatty had given her and always wore it with such pride. One of those people that she allowed such freedom in her home convinced her to take the ring off when she went to the hospital and they would see to it that it was kept safe for her. After Minta's death that ring never surfaced again.

What an honor it was to get to know a lady who was a star in another era from mine and who conducted herself as a star to her very last breath.

THE KID

The silent era of motion pictures did have a number of juvenile players, but few attained super stardom like Shirley Temple did in the '30s. The one that came the closest would have been Mary Pickford, known as America's Sweetheart, but the fact of the matter was that Mary did not join the film industry until she was about 16 years old and was portraying a child into her thirties. Admittedly, she had the look of a child, being very petite in form with long golden curls and eyes that registered the innocence of youth, but years later the public only accepted the concept of the child star when they truly were children.

There was one child who managed to attain stardom in the silent era. It was not a girl but a boy with an angelic face, big brown eyes, and a tremendous talent for pathos way beyond his tender years. His name was Jackie Coogan.

Jackie accomplished the near impossible by just about stealing the 1921 movie *The Kid* away from the genius Charlie Chaplin but because Mr. Chaplin had great respect for his little co-star, it was with his blessings that Jackie was taken into the hearts of the American public.

I never met Jackie until we were both adults. It was 1979 and we were asked to co-emcee the very first Youth in Film award show. It was a mimic of the Oscar ceremony, but with the distinction that all of the nominees were kid actors. Although Jackie was quite a number of years older than me, I certainly was aware that he was a very important part of

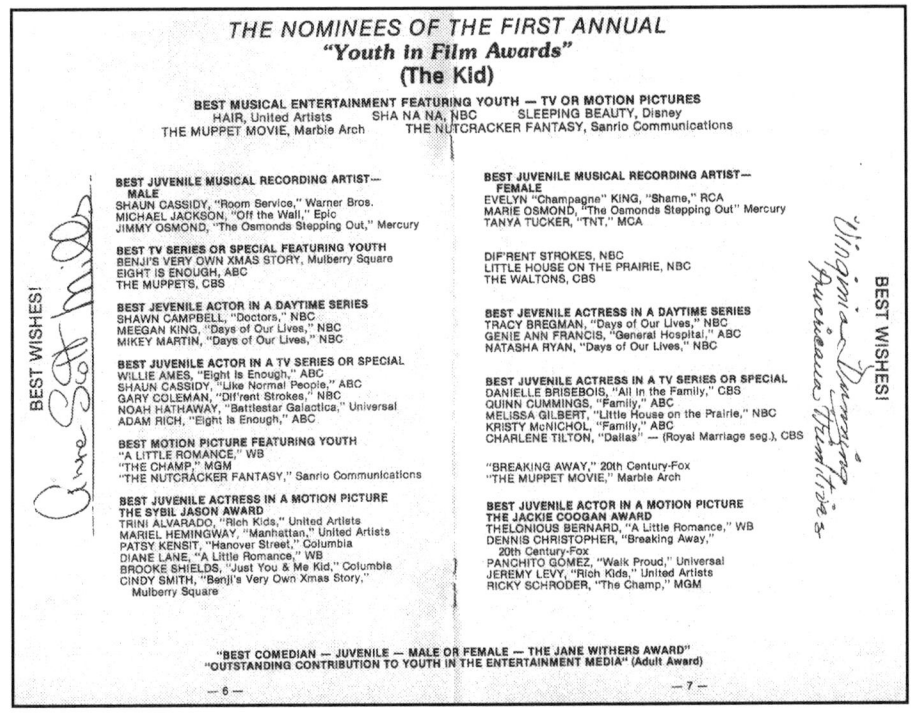

The nominees for the Sybil Jason Award are...

the history of motion pictures. However, by 1979, television audiences knew him best for *The Addams Family* sitcom, where he portrayed a character known as Uncle Fester Frump.

Although children were known to have given wonderful performances in motion pictures they were never nominated for an Oscar. It's true some were given a mini-Oscar as a tribute to their talent but this was just a form of tokenism. Thankfully, years later this was changed to a degree and a select few attained full status as Oscar winners. However, in 1979, Youth in Film was a step in the right direction in that it spotlighted the talents of the young actor and made them the main target of appreciation, while only having to compete with their contemporaries.

I helped the Youth in Film committee by getting in touch with some of my contemporaries to act as presenters of the awards to the new kid stars and I was especially proud that one of the categories was called the Sybil Jason Drama Award for Best Actress. Secretly I was hoping that little Diane Lane would win it for *A Little Romance* and she did and I am the least surprised person that she went on to become a very successful mature actress in the contemporary Hollywood of today.

I enjoyed working with Jackie, although I was quite surprised to find him a very quiet person. It was during rehearsals of us announcing the ex-child star presenters that I wondered if he had a bad back because he didn't wait for the presenter to come up to the podium on cue, but took the nearest chair just off the stage area to rest. However, quiet or not, it never failed to bring a huge grin to his face every time I kidded him mercilessly about him starting the fad of the Dutch boy hairdo that we girl child stars took on as our own.

One of the things that I liked best about Jackie was his love for his family. I personally fell in love with his grandson, who looked so very much like his grandfather did at that same age and he seemed to thoroughly enjoy turning up to all of the rehearsals.

I must say that the show itself was fun to do and we got a lot of positive coverage from the trade papers about it.

It was not more than a week or two after the awards show that I received an invitation to Jackie's 65th birthday party, to be held at the famous Brown Derby on Vine Street in Hollywood on October 26, 1979.

Jackie just glowed with the adulation that was paid to him at the party and none other than Geraldo Rivera arrived with a television crew and did coverage of all of us gathered around Jackie.

A week later I received a very cute thank you note for attending his birthday party.

Besides out similar kid hairdos we had something else in common that spanned the years. When I left Warner Bros. and before Twentieth Century-Fox signed me to a contract, I did a movie called *Woman Doctor* that was directed by a charming man named Sidney Salkow. Jackie agreed that it was a pleasure working with this director because he helmed several segments of *The Addams Family*, which included the one that focused on Jackie's character, Uncle Fester. Many years later when I read that Sidney had passed away, I got in touch with his widow and told her how very fond I had been of her husband.

The last time that I was in contact with Jackie must have been around the beginning of 1984. He had always been upset that there were still huge loopholes in the Coogan Law that was supposed to protect the earnings of the kid stars from mismanagement of their money. Of course, I am sure that Jackie must have gotten in touch with other ex-child stars, but I am speaking for myself when I say that I received a phone call from him asking me whether I would accompany him to Washington because he wanted to present the problems and possible solutions to the powers that be in Congress. I told him that he could count on me, but that never came to pass. Jackie died on March 1, 1984 and although there have been valiant attempts to close up the holes in the Coogan Law, kids' earnings are still in jeopardy to this day.

I am delighted to say that the tradition of acting is being carried on by his grandson, Keith Coogan, who I am sure some of you have seen in movies such as 1995's *Downhill Willie* and 1991's *Don't Tell Mom the Babysitter's Dead*, which is often shown on television. Jackie would have been so proud that his son is a writer, and his grandson proudly carries on the name of Coogan on film to this day.

Vaudevillians Supreme

MIKE and MEYER

Nineteen Thirty-eight was a brand-new start for me in more ways than one.

My last movie under contract to Warner Bros. was finished and in the can and I had been signed to do a movie called *Woman Doctor,* starring Henry Wilcoxon as my father, Frieda Inescort doing a repeat as my mother (she was my mother in *The Great O'Malley*) and Claire Dodd as the "other woman," as she also had portrayed in the Warner Bros. movie I had co-starred in with Al Jolson, *The Singing Kid.*

In the middle of production of *Woman Doctor* both MGM and Twentieth Century-Fox offered me a long-term contract to their studio. Ultimately, my new agent opted for Fox.

However, before any of the above happened, a court case against my uncle-guardian was brought to a conclusion by the judge that handled the case in which he banished my uncle from America. It was for the misappropriation of a great deal of my earnings in which he slowly siphoned the money out of the country into England. There is no doubt that at one time I was very fond of my uncle, but he was an extreme disciplinarian, completely self-involved and although it had always been my sister Anita who had taught me everything that I knew in a gentle and patient way, my uncle was quite delusional in thinking that he was responsible for my talents and for my career.

Regardless of the situation, it was a very sad parting when he left to go back to England, but I guess old habits die hard because he took with him three other pressbooks of mine, every home movie that we took with celebrities, a lot of studio photographs and jewelry that was given to me by Al Jolson and Louella Parsons.

After he left, Anita and I certainly didn't need the trappings of the likes of the Sunset Boulevard house so opted for an apartment in Beverly Hills right near the Fox Studios. Even if we had wanted to continue living in our house on Sunset we couldn't have because my uncle sold it on my behalf but pocketed the money so the decision was actually made for us.

Although my sister was very careful about my security, for the very first time in my life I felt like a very normal kid. I was able to make friends with our neighbors and to ride my brand-new bike around the neighborhood with check-ins with Anita every hour or so. In our apartment building, with just one wall separating our two apartments, our neighbor was Douglas Fairbanks Jr. and his wife, at that time, Mary. He was absolutely charming, very handsome and Anita and I saw each of them on a daily basis. Years later, what puzzled me when I read Doug's autobiography was his version of where he was when the news came that England had just gone to war with Germany. He mentioned that he was on a yacht with Ronald Colman and that they weighed anchor as soon as the news came through and headed back to LA. In actuality it was morning when we first heard the war news and the people in our apartment building started gathering in the hallways to discuss what was going on. Doug and Mary were still in their robes and when I mentioned that I was taking my bike to pickup a newspaper at the store they asked me to kindly pick them up a copy as well.

The last time that I saw Doug was about eight years ago at a nostalgia event honoring those of us of the Golden Era of motion pictures.

A lovely photo was taken of Doug, Buddy Rogers, myself and many others. I hope one day to be able to track that photo down because it was truly historical in nature. Many stars that represented various eras of the history of Hollywood (not just the Golden Era) posed for that picture and I think it would fascinate any historian.

I really enjoyed my neighborhood and made a lot of friends of the people that lived in the surrounding area. Two people that I was particularly fond of was a very old couple who treated me like a much loved grandchild. They just lived a block away from us and when I told Anita that they had invited me to lunch at their apartment she said that she would like to meet them first. She did and fell in love with both of them. It got to the point that I made a daily visit to them and they looked as forward to my visits as I did to visiting them. There didn't seem to be any differentiation in age because our conversations were mutually fascinating in that I learned that he had been in show business too. Usually when this dear little man told me all about his experiences in show business his wife always served me my favorite dessert that my grandmother used to fix for me in London…tapioca pudding, but the tapioca was giant sized just like my grandmother used to fix.

I remember one day vividly that the old gentleman mentioned that if I thought that Lana Turner was a beauty she had nothing on Lillian Russell. I couldn't believe my ears as I knew that she was a woman that was unbelievably famous more years ago than I could count. He and his partner had worked with her and just as he said that, there came a knock on their front door and it was his partner coming to visit them. You never saw two men so much unalike as Joe Weber and Lew Fields. My friend Joe Weber was just about my size and Mr. Fields towered over both of us. I really was amused to see that they still played off each other even though they had retired from show business decades ago. They practiced camaraderie in the finest sense of the word because when I asked what kind of an act they did, as if on cue, they asked me if I'd like to see what they did. They went right into their act that mainly consisted of Mr. Fields abusing

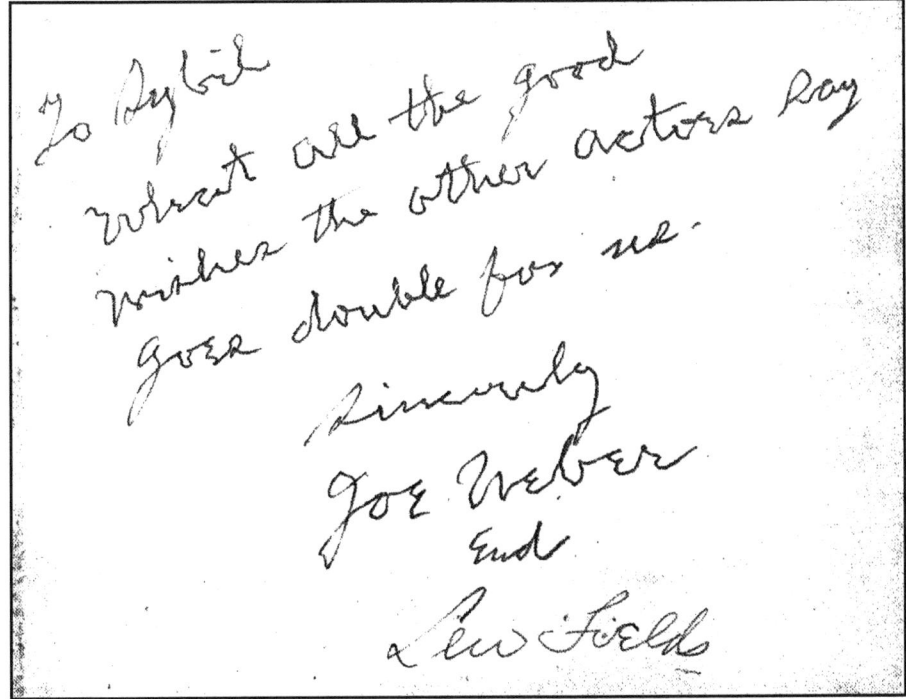

Weber & Fields' autographs.

Mr. Weber and continually pushing him and when he had his limit the little man would strain his neck to look up at his partner and say (and audiences waited for this), "Don't pooosh me, Meyer, don't pooosh me!!!" I just couldn't stop laughing to see these two wonderful men go into their act as if they had an audience of hundreds and had never stopped doing their act for the public!!

I was just about to start the production of *The Little Princess* when Anita found a much larger apartment located a lot nearer to Fox so reluctantly I said goodbye to my dear friends and promised them that I would visit them again when the movie was finished. I missed my daily visits with Joe and Lillian Weber and even though I kept my promise to go see them after *The Little Princess* was finished, somehow it was never the same again and we only saw each other a few more times after that. In the next two years many things had changed for all of us. After I had finished doing *The Bluebird* at Fox I was sent on a worldwide tour and couldn't come back to the States because the frightening attack on Pearl Harbor had occurred and now the United States was also in the war and my parents did not want me to go back to America during wartime. I also learned, much to my sadness, that Mr. Fields had died on July 20, 1941 and dear little Mr. Weber had passed away in May 1942. I tried to contact some people in America to find out what happened to Mrs. Lillian Weber, but nobody seemed to know.

But to this day I will always remember Lillian and Joe Weber and Lew Fields with great affection and to have had the honor to have been their lone audience for their act one fine day in Beverly Hills in 1938.

Dem Guys

The first movie that I did for Warner Bros in 1935 was *Little Big Shot* and although it was very similar to my friend Shirley Temple's *Little Miss Marker*, luckily it was well received.

It had a wonderful cast and a first-class director in Michael Curtiz. One of the reasons that this movie really helped to launch me as Warner Bros.' first child star in the eyes of the public was that the whole cast worked so well together.

Glenda Farrell ultimately became a good and close friend after the movie was in the can and the irrepressible scene-stealer Edward Everett Horton was later cast in the 1936 movie *The Singing Kid* that co-starred me with superstar Al Jolson and it was much fun reuniting with Ed.

In 1933 Robert Armstrong had a huge success in *King Kong* and I was a fortunate little girl to get such magnificent backing in my first movie for Warners. I must say that a lot of attention was given to me and Bob Armstrong in our dramatic scenes together. One in particular was significantly pointed out in the reviews as a real heart-tugger, as well as in its complete believability in context. Bob's character wants to abandon me so he takes me to an orphanage where he intends to leave me. As soon as I realize what's happening I beg him not to leave me there but to take me with him. After the scene was over Bob told my sister Anita that he could barely "hold it together" while doing that scene with me because he couldn't imagine anyone leaving a child so sensitive and quietly emotional as I portrayed in that scene.

Besides the main characters, *Little Big Shot* had a great cast of "heavies" in it as well. To name the most prominent of them was J. Carrol Naish, Marc Lawrence, Jack LaRue, Ward Bond and Joseph Sawyer.

86 Five Minutes More

Glenda Farrel and self.

To see any of these gentlemen in the movies you just knew that trouble was ahead for their "victims." In person they couldn't have been nicer. And gentler. When the movie is screened nowadays at different venues, one can hear a collective murmur coming from the audience when they spot Ward Bond. He barely had a line to say in the whole movie so I would venture a guess that this was one of his first appearances onto the screen. Believe it or not, out of the four "heavies," he was the most shy. He didn't seem to pal around with the rest of "the boys" in between scenes;

not because he was unfriendly, but simply because he was not that self confident as yet. Remember, this was light years away from *Wagon Train*!

J. Carrol Naish was a very dedicated actor and most friendly to everyone, yet he was on the quiet side and preferred to study his script and observe all the other scenes being shot with other cast members. He seemed particularly interested in the methods of direction that Michael Curtiz used.

Joseph Sawyer socialized with everyone and seemed to be enjoying himself in between scenes portraying one of the henchmen in the movie. It was kind of funny to see that he had a very healthy appetite and if there was a morsel of food within yards of him he most certainly would find it!

I enjoyed being with all of these actors, but my two favorites were Jack LaRue and Marc Lawrence. Being a polite little English girl, I was brought up to never stare at a person who had a "different look" to them, but I was absolutely fascinated by the pockmarks on Marc's face. I had never seen pockmarks before but in movies it sure added to his menace appeal. I *never* felt menaced by Marc mainly because when he heard a funny story his whole face would break out in a huge grin and doubly so if he was the one telling a joke and got a good reaction. However, he did have another side to him. If a person got out of line with Marc or with someone that he liked, the menace came out in him and, believe me, the offending party would tread lightly. Of course, these were people who didn't have a clue that Marc was really just a pussy cat. I saw this when we would bump into each other when we attended autograph parties at these nostalgia gatherings in the 2000s. The fans would approach him very gingerly hoping not to "ruffle his feathers," not realizing that he enjoyed being recognized.

In fact, he traveled all over the United States attending these autograph gatherings as a guest star for many years. We did stay in contact but only through phone calls and letters, because his home was in Palm Springs and he only left it when he had a part in a movie or attended various functions. Marc was content with his life and bless him he remained pretty well active until his death in 2005 at the age of 95!

My husband Tony and I had our home in Studio City and we often took walks up to Ventura Boulevard. We knew most of the restaurants around our neighborhood, but there was one Italian one we had never tried. Tony was not Italian but he loved Italian food so one evening we decided to try this one out. The restaurant was very busy and because we had not made any reservations the matre d' suggested we wait our turn at the bar. As we sat down and ordered our drinks Tony and I got into a conversation about a certain movie we had seen years before but couldn't quite remember who starred in it. We both thought it might have been Alan Ladd and we no sooner said this when a voice at my elbow announced, "It *was* Alan Ladd."

I turned to look at the man sitting next to me and I almost fell off my seat. He had not changed that much from 1935 so I knew who he was straight away. It was Jack LaRue himself!! When I explained who I was he couldn't believe that I was grown up enough to be an old married lady. We did our best to update each other and he told my husband what a terrific little actress I had been and could never understand why I hadn't continued on with my career. By this time our table was ready and we asked Jack if he would be our guest for dinner. He thanked us and said that he couldn't but would join us for a short while at our table. I was sorry when he had to leave but by the time our dinner was over I saw that he hadn't left the restaurant so I fully intended to go over and say our goodbyes

Tony asked for the check but our waiter told him that it had been taken care of by the owner. We were puzzled by this generosity so asked our waiter to point him out to us so that we could thank him. The waiter pointed to Jack!!

Jack LaRue.

He was the owner of that Italian restaurant and obviously got a big kick out of our surprised looks. When we went over to thank him, he assured us that it had been his pleasure and that he hoped that we would visit him again.

And we did…several times…until one day we noticed that his Italian restaurant had now become an oriental one and the new owners didn't have Jack's address. Sadly, we lost touch with him for a number of years until I was asked by author Richard Lamparski to appear at a book signing for his newest book at the Beverly Wilshire Hotel in Beverly Hills. A lot of us ex-child stars of both movies and television were seated together at a long table to autograph Richard's book in the sections where we individually appeared and the attendance of the public was very brisk.

I happened to look up when there was a lull in the line of people waiting for autographs and at a separate table away from our "kiddie section" was my valued friend of many years, Jack LaRue. He had aged considerably by then but he still had that lovely twinkle in his eye and was enjoying every moment of the attention he was getting from his fans. I had a feeling that he was probably suffering from some form of arthritis because he never rose up from his chair all the time the event was going on.

I never saw Jack again. We heard that he had passed away in Santa Monica in January of 1984, at the age of 82.

He may have been known as one of the greatest "hoods" that enriched the Warner Brothers gangster movies but to me he was always a lovely and gracious gentleman.

I think that a very interesting sidelight to this story of the people who were involved with the movie *Little Big Shot* is that there *was* a later scene in the interior of the "orphanage" where my character eventually wound up as an orphan. The head mistress there was played by the wonderful character actress Emma Dunn and, as her assistant (who had a very small part) was a woman who, in real life, was an integral part of the history of vaudeville. Her name was Mary Foy and she was one of the kids of the famous Foy family and years later Bob Hope portrayed their father Eddie Foy in the movie *The Seven Little Foys*.

It is one of life's strange coincidences that when I made four Technicolor shorts for Warner Bros., one of the producers was Bryan Foy, who went on to become the casting director at Twentieth Century-Fox when I was under contract there and making the *Little Princess* and *The Blue Bird* with Shirley Temple.

Second Banana Scene Stealers

I cannot think of two finer scene stealers than the irrepressible "Double Take" and "put upon" character actor Edward Everett Horton and the gruff but completely lovable perennial sidekick Allen Jenkins. I was fortunate to have worked with Ed Horton in my first movie for Warners, *Little Big Shot,* in 1935 and then once again in 1936 in *The Singing Kid*, in which I co-starred with the superstar Al Jolson. In the latter movie, Allen played Ed's "not-quite-playing-with-a-full-deck" sidekick to perfection and their timing throughout the movie was impeccable. One of the most fun scenes in the movie for me to do was where Allen is teaching me how to play onesies twosies, more familiarly known as Jacks. I had a hard time keeping a straight face watching him play his character in a child-like immature way!! But, more about Allen later on.

I think just about everyone at one time or other thought that Edward Everett Horton was British, but he was far from that, having been born in Brooklyn, New York. However, he was definitely an Anglophile and took frequent trips to England, which you will soon see became very important to me.

As I have explained once before a gentleman by the name of Irving Asher was head of the Warner Bros. studio in London in early 1935 and when I appeared on the Palladium and the Royal Albert Hall stages he ordered it to be photographed and used it as a screen test to send it to Jack Warner in Hollywood with the enquiry whether they could use this talented little girl at the studio. Ed Horton happened to be in London at that time and Mr. Asher asked him if he would do him the favor of taking a reel of film over to Hollywood and delivering it to Jack Warner. He was leaving for the States by ship in a few days' time anyway and said he would be glad to comply with Asher's wishes.

Later on we found out that Ed didn't know what was in that can of film and it was just one of those coincidences that it turned out that after Jack Warner viewed the test and he cabled Irving Asher "Sign her" that Edward Everett Horton was assigned to my very first movie in Hollywood called *Little Big Shot.*

I loved his sense of dry humor and he marveled at the fact that a child as young as I was did not let his subtleties "go over my head." For some strange reason I understood him at all times and he was completely amused by it. One day he was trying to explain in his very unique way what happened a few months ago to him and the gentleman he was telling it to just "didn't get it." *Very* annoyed, Mr. Horton pointed to me and said, "Ask her. She'll explain it to you"!!

When we were on location, Ed loved just sitting back in his director's chair and observing everything around him. I did a bit of math the other day and came up with the fact that he must have been around fifty years old when we made that movie. Now to a child, fifty is rather old and so it was mind boggling to me when he talked about one of his favorite subjects, his mother…who lived with him! She passed away when she was 100 years old and I remember people taking bets that Edward Everett Horton would give her a run for her money in regards to age. Unfortunately, for all of his fans, he died in 1970 at the age of 84.

ALLEN JENKINS

On location of *The Singing Kid* the biggest jokester of them all was Allen Jenkins and Al Jolson loved palling around with him. Allen was always first in line for the box lunches and he did an amazing repartee every day using his food as props!!! Sometimes our director had to remind everyone that lunch was over and so was the show (meaning Allen) and that it was time to get back to work.

But even Jolie one time said, "Waida minute…waida minute…he still has a fruit to do!!"

After we finished *The Singing Kid,* I used to see Allen every now and again on the lot going from soundstage to soundstage. He was the busiest actor in town and sometimes worked three movies simultaneously!!

It was many years till I saw him again. It happened that a theater on Hollywood Boulevard that specialized in showing "old movies" was showing *The Singing Kid* and the manager-owner asked Allen and me to attend as guest stars. Allen hadn't changed and neither had his enthusiasm for

Allen Jenkins, Al Jolson, me and Edward Everett Horton in *The Singing Kid*.

life. We had so much fun that night and bounced around a lot of memories, much to my husband's delight. As usually happens when you haven't seen someone for a while, with all good intentions you promise each other to stay in touch but unfortunately that didn't happen. But we did have another meeting in 1974.

Tony and I loved to take walks around the Santa Monica business Promenade and one Saturday afternoon I saw a man that vaguely looked like Allen but I wasn't sure so didn't approach him. He noticed me looking at him and finally he approached us and said, "Sybil?" It *was* Allen, but he had gotten quite old and didn't look at all well. There were nice benches around so we took one and he explained that his son had a jewelry store and that he used to visit it quite often. I assumed that Allen was semi-retired and was enjoying his free time, but I don't think there was any enjoyment there. He admitted that he missed all the excitement of moviemaking, but by 1974 things had changed in the business and they didn't want "old codgers like me." It was so sad to hear him talk like that because that was so unlike feisty Allen Jenkins. However, we did spend a lovely afternoon together and just before Tony and I said our goodbyes to him he asked me if I had any photos of all of us from *The Singing Kid*. When I told him that I did, amazingly, he said that he didn't have one

Allen and I at the Bijous Theatre when they showed *The Singing Kid*.

scrap of anything to show his grandkids from all his years in show business. I promised to make him copies of everything that I had on him and as soon as I got it all together we would meet again so that I could give it to him.

He left the Promenade with a smile on his face. As promised in two weeks time I not only had made copies of all the stills that I had from *The Singing Kid*, but I found old movie magazines that had his pictures in them.

I could only imagine how that was going to perk him up but suddenly I came to the realization that we didn't get his home address. Tony reminded me that Allen had pointed out his son's jewelry shop and that we could leave the package there for him. When we got there, the store was closed…permanently. We tried to make enquiries where to reach his son but no one had any information that we could use. It couldn't have been too long after our last visit with Allen when we noticed in the obituaries in the newspaper that he had died in Santa Monica in that year of 1974.

There is no doubt in my mind that Edward Everett Horton and Allen Jenkins were tops as second banana scene-stealers and how fortunate I was to have worked with two such great gentlemen who were much more than any character they ever portrayed on film.

Us "Kids"

BEFORE AND AFTER

This chapter is much more "after" than "before" because I did not grow up with my Hollywood contemporaries in the years of World War II because I was living in South Africa at that time. It is a rather unusual story that I covered in *My Fifteen Minutes*.

However, a lot of us became friendly once we were all young adults because we would meet on a regular basis when many organizations arranged banquets to pay tribute to our careers that were at their height during Hollywood's Golden Era of the '30s and '40s.

You will see that some of these relationships were of short terms due to various factors. However, fortunately, others developed into lifelong friendships that are ongoing to this day and are no less treasured because they were developed in our adult years rather than in our youth.

I have a good example of a very short relationship that occurred in 1938 when Shirley Temple and I were in the midst of production of *The Little Princess* at Twentieth Century-Fox. Even though there were many kid actresses portraying boarding school students at "nasty Miss Minchin's School for Girls," we very rarely socialized with each other. This was not because of an unfriendly attitude from either the girls or myself but simply because we did not have any scenes together. When I was busy, they weren't needed on the set and vice versa. About the only girl that I spent any amount of time with besides Shirley was Marcia Mae Jones. She was the unfortunate little actress who memorably got fireside ashes dumped over her head by Shirley in the movie.

However, the very short-term acquaintance that I made during this time had nothing to do with the movie.

There was a very good restaurant on the studio lot called the Café De Paris and my sister Anita and I had lunch there every day. We never had to wait for a table because the manager always had one reserved for us. This was not an unusual courtesy. It was a policy that had a purpose to it. For those of us who were in production of a movie, sometimes we were on a very short break from filming and had to get back to the set. If we had had to wait for a table, we probably would not have had time to eat lunch.

The Café de Paris was a large restaurant and Shirley, when she was younger, celebrated birthdays in a certain part of the Café that was closed off from the main room. The menu was varied and very good but on her birthdays they always served her favorite food at that time, which was creamed tuna on a pastry shell.

On this particular day in 1938 I had a whole hour for lunch so Anita and I took our time eating our meal. The restaurant was packed and the noise level was high but mid-meal we saw a man and a young woman wend their way through the crowd and stopping at just about every table for a moment or two. When they got to our table the man, who was from the publicity department, introduced the young woman as the studio's newest contract player. She was lovely with dark hair and gorgeous dark expressive eyes.

She seemed very shy and looked like she just wanted the earth to open up and swallow her, but underneath that sense of panic she had a very sweet personality. She acknowledged us and said that she was so pleased to meet everyone that up until now she had only enjoyed on the screen. The man informed us that she would be starting work on her first movie for Fox momentarily and felt that it wouldn't be too long before everyone would know of Fox's newest little starlet.

I didn't see her again until a week or two later. I had been asked to have some stills taken that could be used for publicity purposes and when Anita and I got to the very small set, which was used for shooting these stills, the new little actress was there for the same reason. She greeted my sister and me in a very friendly way but it was obvious that she was feeling very uncomfortable about the poses she was asked to take for her pictures. I would say so!! They had her in an ultra-sophisticated dress which belied the freshness of her natural self and were posing her draped on a chaise lounge. She told my sister that she didn't like her dress or her too heavy makeup and she didn't know who to complain to. We were not in the position to give her advice because I wasn't treated the same way that I had been at Warner Bros. and it was obvious by the treatment I was getting from Mr. Zanuck that I was nothing more than an inconvenience to him. However, Anita did suggest that perhaps she should have a talk with the publicity man who had escorted her around the Café de Paris.

Imagine our shock when we later found out that this young actress only *looked* like a woman, but in reality was only a bit over fifteen years of age and only four years older than Shirley and me at that time!! It gave me the shivers to think the unlikely happening that in a short four more years that they could have Shirley or me playing romantic parts with grown-up men!! Of course, little did I know or for that matter did Shirley, that in a short *six* years time she would, in real life, be married to a very handsome young soldier, John Agar!

With John Agar at a western party.

But getting back to our young actress...The publicity man had been correct when he said it would not be long before everyone would know who she was. She went from being leading lady opposite one of Fox's most handsome leading men, Tyrone Power, to characters that were portrayed as *femme fatales*. One of her most memorable characters was as the "wrong side of the tracks," disgruntled wife of Paul Douglas in the movie *A Letter to Three Wives*. Of course, I am talking about Linda Darnell. I only saw

Linda one more time and that was at the premier showing of *The Little Princess*. By that time she looked like she was "comfortable" in her new persona!!

Tragically, Linda died at the age of 42. She had been visiting some friends back east and one night, after watching one of her very first movies on television, she retired to the bedroom of the townhouse she was staying in. It caught fire and Linda died two days later at a hospital from severe burns.

Our acquaintanceship was very short, but my memory is long about the fresh-looking young girl who had visions of a big career to look forward to.

WHAT YOU SEE IS WHAT YOU GET

1938-1939 was a strange and sometimes frightening period in my life. Strange, because I was no longer at Warner Bros., yet busy making a movie that was one of the first non-western productions at Republic Studios. It was called *Woman Doctor* and had a wonderful cast, producer and director. After the movie was in the can and I had received such good reviews Fox offered me a contract to join their studio. The signing had not yet taken place because my manager was mulling over whether to take the offer from MGM, who had also offered a contract to me, or to Fox.

But before that happened I experienced the absolute worst happening in my life at that time. As everyone knows, my sister Anita was the world to me. She was mother figure, mentor, sister, and the best friend I ever had. One day she became very ill with a life-threatening condition which demanded an operation of an extreme nature immediately. We had no relatives in this country but fortunately my tutor at Warner Bros. had become an extremely good friend of my sister and myself throughout my years at Warners. Lois Horn was a no-nonsense type of woman with a heart of gold who soon took over my care with ease and determination, which in itself eased Anita's mind to a great degree.

[scan0035 upper left, caption: With Lois Horn, on the rooftop of my Hollywood Hills home. The man was a Warners dance coach.]

My sister survived her long and intricate operation, but she was in intensive care because it was touch and go for a while there and then in recuperation for an even longer period before she was finally released from the hospital. Lois made sure that we visited Anita daily. I will never forget the time when my sister was under an oxygen tent and when Lois and I entered the room Anita lifted her head up to greet us. It tore me up in pieces to see her like this, but she soon had me smiling. Anita was just being Anita and on patrol duty when she told Lois that my socks needed pulling up! As long as I can remember I have had an idiosyncrasy that exists to this day that when I wear socks and after only a short while the heel portion slides down into my shoes. I never used to be aware that this was happening until I felt Anita tugging my socks back up again where they belonged.

I just wrote that Lois and I visited Anita daily in the hospital. To be precise I should have said that we saw her in the early evenings. Lois was still tutoring at Warners and because I could not be left alone she carted me off with her in the mornings to the studio.

Lois's student was a young lady of 16 years of age and the law required that she still put in three hours of school work before she was legally accepted as an adult. It seemed so incongruous to me that, after doing a love scene with a man who was 24 years older than she was, she would join Lois and me to do battle with math problems! By now you may have guessed I am talking about Joan Leslie, who played Gary Cooper's wife in the now-famous movie *Sergeant York*.

With Lois Horn, on the rooftop of my Hollywood Hills home. The man was a Warners dance coach.

May I say that one cannot help but love Joan Leslie? She was the sweetest thing on two feet then and she has not changed one iota now. What you see is what you get from Ms. Leslie. Along with that sweetness there is a great sense of humor. I will never forget what she taught me in between scenes of *Sergeant York*. Joan was studying German at that time and she tutored me how to say "I love you with all of my heart" in that language. But she put a spin on it. After she said that romantic sentence she would draw one side of her upper lip to the left and the lower lip to the right to finish off her funny routine!! I aced it after a few tries and never forgot it. Years later I had told my dear husband Tony all about my experience with Joan so when I introduced him to her after she and I met for the first time in years he asked if we still remembered what she taught me. Right on cue we *both* went into the German and ended it off with the lip trick as if it were just yesterday. In this day and age we meet quite often at various showbiz functions and share a lot of laughs. If you are a fan of

Joan, you might be happy to know that she doesn't need a lot of makeup to look beautiful. She *is* beautiful inside and out and if you are lucky enough to bump into her at some of these autograph signings she will greet you with a big smile and a warm word or two. That would be no act.

That would be Joan Leslie!!

At a signing with Jonathan Winters (above) and Carl Ballantine (below).

Honored at a Cinecon banquet in September 2006, with Rose Marie (above) and Tab Hunter (left).

Ben Lyon and myself being honored at a banquet.

With Tom Drake at a banquet at the Fox & Hounds.

Together again with Gale Sondergard (*The Blue Bird*).

With Mario Lanza's son.

With ex-child star. David Holt.

The studio dedicated a whole day and night to me, attended by my fan club members who flew in from around the USA and overseas, 2004.

Marquee of the famous Roxy Theatre in NY.

Gene Raymond and myself at the banquet of a Jeanette MacDonald fan club.

With Tommy Farrell (Glenda's son).

Kathryn Grayson and me at a tribute party.

HOW LUCKY CAN YOU GET

I find myself in a very fortunate position. It is such a treat when I get together with very special people who are generous, warm and so giving that it seems only natural to follow my last story on Joan Leslie with this next one.

When I was in Africa during World War II, I never gave up the enjoyable habit of going to the movies. In Africa we got all of the latest British movies that really weren't shown in the United States until right after the war and, of course, there were the movies starring so many of the people that I had worked with during my career at Warners and Fox Studios. Some times that was hard for me emotionally.

I would have loved to have continued on with my acting career and perhaps worked once again with all of these people I was now viewing on the screen thousands of miles away from Hollywood…but that was not to be.

Apart from the stars I was personally acquainted with, there were also movies that starred people I had never met that I never missed the chance of seeing in their latest productions. I remember almost falling off my seat with laughter at the antics of Red Skelton when he did his "Guzzlers Gin" routine. To me there was nothing funnier at that time. Of course, I had my dramatic favorites like Bette Davis, Ingrid Bergman, Claude Rains, Spencer Tracy and many others that I wouldn't miss seeing in their latest productions. But then there were the typical teenage musical or comedy films that I enjoyed because, after all, I was also a teenager at that time. I never missed the Donald O'Connor-Peggy Ryan movies, or the Deanna Durbin or Gloria Jean productions, and then who could forget the Andy Hardy series!! I got quite a kick out of seeing my friend Lana Turner playing the *femme fatale* to Mickey Rooney's Andy Hardy character. However, I especially loved it when they featured sweet little Polly Benedict, a.k.a. Miss Ann Rutherford. I thought that she was the cutest thing on two feet. You know what…I still do. Just like Joan Leslie, "What you see is what you get"!!

I never met Ann until I was an adult but you would never know it. She has the facility to make you feel as if you've known each other your whole life. I also have never met anyone that loyal or that fair like she is to most of her friends.

I met Ann at a party that a contemporary of mine was holding. It was a very unique party in that only ex-child stars were invited to attend. To be very honest with the reader, that night I felt a bit "out of it" because I had not grown up with most of my contemporaries and unfortunately I was made to feel that way by quite a few of the attendees. When my husband and I first arrived at the party our hostess and her husband owned a rather big apartment building in Beverly Hills and when several of us were going up in the elevator to their penthouse apartment I happened to make the remark that this party would be the closest any of us would ever come to a high school reunion. Amongst others in the elevator (and there were quite a few others) Ann Rutherford seemed to get a big kick out of the remark and thoroughly agreed that that's exactly how it felt. I had reason later on in the evening to be very grateful to her. The party was held on the main floor in the apartment's garden area and I had fun meeting many "kids" I had not met but admired before. They all looked wonderful and very glamorous and I really envied them their camaraderie that I could not fully share in. However, most of us were or had been married and at least had that in common. I had known Bonita Granville in the old days when she was going steady with Jackie Cooper, but that evening I was introduced to her husband, William Wrather, who my husband and I became quite fond of.

The same went for Margaret O'Brien and her husband, Roy Thorsen, who I often see at these nostalgia events to this day. Unfortunately, they are no longer married but it's lovely to see that they are the best of friends. But I am getting away from what a special human being Ann Rutherford is.

At a Hawaiian party with Margaret O'Brien and Donald O'Connor.

After everyone had socialized at the beginning of the evening a lot of great entertainment had been arranged and we were all in for a real treat!!! The entertainment consisted of some of our contemporaries. Imagine seeing Donald O'Connor and his oft-sidekick Sidney Miller doing a musical number, Jane Powell singing so beautifully and the list went on and on. One by one everyone was called up to the microphone and said a word or two and I was a bit surprised to hear several of the stars say that their friend "so and so" said the most delightful truism earlier in the evening that this would be the closest any of us would come to a high school reunion. Being quite human I did feel very hurt by this until Ann Rutherford got up and said, "As Sybil Jason said at the very beginning of this evening..." and she quoted me word for word. As the years have gone by, I have found out that this is typical of the kind of person Ann Rutherford is. I know that she is this compassionate to all of her friends, new and old alike. Each year most of us have attended a nostalgia event called The Jivin' Jacks and Jills and it's an event Tony and I always looked forward to as we would see all of our old friends there. Ann is always surrounded by fans and friends alike and she deserves every kudo that she receives. The very first year that I attended without my dear husband of almost 58 years, who had lost his valiant fight with lung cancer, Annie insisted that I and my daughter Toni sit at her reserved table. She is not the type to get maudlin but you know she cares and cares deeply if one of her friends is dealing with a loss.

Just like Joan Leslie, if you were to bump into Ann Rutherford she too would greet you with a warm smile, and a happy word or two and be gracious and thank you for asking for her autograph.

Ann looks great for *any* age and if you spotted her on the street you would certainly recognize her because she still has that Polly Benedict look if just a wee bit more mature now.

I honestly don't know of another star that is as down to earth as Annie is. She may drive a Rolls-Royce (and she does and gets kidded good-naturedly about it,) but she is the type to call 'em as she sees 'em and that is marvelous because you always know where you stand with Ann Rutherford. Everyone should have an Ann Rutherford in their lives.

THE FACE IS FAMILIAR

To this day I have a hard time realizing that I was billed over Humphrey Bogart in a 1937 Warner Bros movie called *The Great O'Malley*. Pat O'Brien starred as James Aloysius O'Malley and I co-starred as the crippled daughter of Humphrey Bogart. It had a wonderful cast, which included such

The Great O'Malley.

stalwart greats as Ann Sheridan, Frieda Inescort and the superb character actor Donald Crisp and the epitome of Irish mothers, Mary Gordon. In my first book I went into detail about the problems that we actors faced during the production due to the idiosyncrasies of our director, William Dieterle, so I won't bore you with a repetition of it. However, quite a few scenes were on the replicated sets of the East Side of New York, as well as the interior and exterior of a school in the same district.

Photographed by ex-child star, Delmar Watson are Peggy Ann Garner, Edith Fellows, Bob Mauch and me at my husband's birthday party.

Quite a number of child extras were used to fill out the scenes of the classroom, street crossing and playground of the school, but there was one particular boy actor who was very well known in movies and he portrayed my very first "boyfriend" named Tubby. His real name was Delmar Watson. All of the nine Watson kids were actors. There were six boys and three girls in the family and Coy, the oldest, headed the list of Gloria, Vivian, Louise, Harry, Billy, Garry, Delmar and lastly Bobs. The three I knew best were Coy, Bobs and most definitely Delmar.

As an adult I made many personal appearances. Some of them were for charitable causes, some were for lecture dates, and others were for miscellaneous show business events. I noticed that just about everywhere I went there was this extremely nice and pleasant photographer. I remember thinking that although I had never met this man before, his face seemed to be so familiar to me, but I figured that that was because I had seen him at so many events that I attended.

How wrong can one person be!!!!

In 1979 my daughter and I were going to give my dear husband, Tony Drake, a surprise birthday party and everything was pretty much hush hush until the big event. While planning it I made a decision that seeing that Tony was familiar with all of us from the 1930s movies it

Bobs Watson, Ann Rutherford and me.

would be exciting for him to meet a lot of them under his own roof. So I got busy sending out invitations to my contemporaries and even those I had just recently met for the first time. I also managed to find the addresses of some of the kids that I worked with in the thirties and invited them too even though I had not seen them in many, many years and wasn't sure whether they'd be interested in attending.

A few days before the party, I had also invited Marvin Paige, who was a casting director at that time and knew just about everyone in town. When he phoned and asked who would be there I read him a list of the people I had invited. He started chuckling when I got to two brothers' names.

Marvin said, "You'll never get them there. They never accept any kind of invitations!!"

Well, he was only half right.

The boys were the twins Bob and Billy Mauch, so famous for their roles in the Warner Bros. movie The *Prince and the Pauper* and it was true that they led very private lives. Billy, at that time, was out of town and couldn't make it, but Bob came and he was just a delight! The three of us were very good friends when we were kids at Warners and went to school together on the lot and their mother was always amazed that I was one of the very few people that could tell the two of them apart.

Our house that night was just packed with fun and memories and our daughter Toni's future husband, Phillip Wayne Rossi, and his father, Frank Wayne (who were producers of the game show *The Price is Right*), brought his wife, Frankie Louise Wayne, and they all just fit right in with everyone else. In fact, Phil had ordered a lookalike telegram gal that did her birthday act for Tony as Mae West, which was a big hit with our crowd and my husband just ate it all up!!!!

Imagine my surprise when the party had just started to get interesting when I opened up my front door and there was that familiar-looking photographer I really had never "met" formally and for a moment I was taken a back. I hadn't invited any photographers or even considered taking photos of our guests myself out of consideration for some of them who might not like their pictures taken at a private party, so I decided no cameras were the order of the night!

That man at the door must have seen my hesitation and that really amused him. He broke out in a grin and said, "I got your invitation, Sybil, and here I am, but you don't have a clue who I am, do you?" He was a real pixie and I was amused because he really got me tagged and I just

Delmar Watson & me.

couldn't wait to find out what he was going to say. Needless to say, I was completely bowled over when he said that he was Delmar Watson and we had worked together on *The Great O'Malley* at Warners in 1937 and here we were a good 43 years later!! What was so very weird is that we had been at so many functions in the present era and I didn't know who he was until now!!! Yes, it is true that I had sent him an invitation, but I hadn't fit the name with that face with a camera that I had seen so often!!! He did take some pictures that night and no one minded because he was "one of us." In fact, the majority of the Watson kids became very famous photographers in their adult years.

After that night Tony, Delmar and I had become good friends and then a few years later when he married a most charming woman named Antoinette our foursome became a real friendship. However, before that happened, Delmar came to the opening of the musical I had composed called *Garage Sale*.

The invited audience was packed with show business people like Fayard Nicholas of the famous dancing Nicholas Brothers, the darling Joan Leslie, and Bonnie Green, who was the widow of my very close friend Johnny Green who had advised me on some of my songs not long

On Delmar's 80th birthday.

before he passed away. Johnny had quite the history. He had been musical director for MGM and won an Academy Award for *Oliver!* and was also the composer of many, many standards, including "Body and Soul" and "I Cover the Waterfront." Also in the audience was Tommy Farrell, Glenda's son, Sidney Miller (Don O'Connor's sidekick and friend in many movies and stage), Giselle MacKenzie, Tony's and my very good friend and famous musician, the NEEM, better known as Henry Nemo, who composed the lovely song "Don't Take Your Love From Me" and was co-composer with Duke Ellington on "I Let a Song Go Out of My Heart." There was also more fabulous icon composers like Henry and Harry Tobias and Richard and Robert Sherman, who had written the fabulous score for *Mary Poppins,* and the list goes on. I am proud to say we had standing room only!! I am also proud to say that on my stage we had some fine names as well. Heading a cast of 14 talented actors and not including the orchestra, the two lead women were Betty Garrett and Carol Bruce. Carol had some wonderful credits to her name. In fact, she was personally chosen by my dear friend "Uncle Jerry" to play Julie in the stage revival of his play, *Show Boat*...Jerome Kern. I had wonderful memories of sitting down at the piano with "Uncle Jerry" when I was a child and played the melody of one of his songs with one finger and he played the base part at his home in Hollywood. However, at the time of *Garage Sale* Carol was known widely for her TV role as the owner of the radio station of *WRKP in Cincinnati*!! As usual, and luckily, Delmar's camera was piping hot that night!!!

Me and Fayard Nicholas doing the light fantastic at a Milton Berle party.

I don't know why Delmar, Tony and I had not established a very close friendship by then, but I suppose it was because we were all busy with our lives and were on the go too much with our various activities. It was almost five years later when we next saw Delmar. After the passing of my dear friend Eleanor Powell a whole group of her closest friends and co-workers gathered to honor her when her star was placed on the Walk of Fame in 1984. I always felt bad that Ellie had not been alive to receive this honor in person because she would have been so proud and, of course, there was no doubt that she deserved it and should have received it many years earlier. However, the main thing is that it was accomplished and there was such a good feeling amongst all of us that day celebrating the life and career of a very dear friend and a great talent…Eleanor Powell… and Delmar was there that day with his camera to commemorate the occasion.

My beloved husband Tony died in 2005, after a valiant fight against lung cancer, and we couldn't quite make our 58th wedding anniversary. About a year after Tony's passing, Antoinette, Delmar and I established a very close friendship. In fact, it started with a surprise birthday party like it had when my daughter and I planned one for Tony a few years back when Delmar knocked on our front door and surprised me.

Good friend and Oscar winner. Johnny Green, composer of "Body and Soul."

Betty Garret and some of the cast of *Garage Sale*.

All of us gathered to honor Ellie Powell's placing a star on the Boulevard, 1984.

Debbie Reynolds, Gene Kelly and myself.

This time it was Antoinette Watson that was going to hold one for Delmar this past year for his eightieth birthday and he had a terrific turnout out of friends and his huge family and their families and as he walked in to the party Antoinette took a picture of us that I like very much because it shows our genuine affection for each other. I thought it was so funny when she asked me permission to use me as an excuse to get him to the party. He doesn't always like to go places but he never misses one that I am attending so she said it was a surprise party to honor me for my career as a child star.

I must mention something of interest to the movie buff. A few years back I attended a barbecue party at the home of Gary Bell, whose partner in the nostalgia movie association of the Jivin' Jacks and Jills, which holds a huge convention once a year in Studio City California, was my friend Michael Fitzgerald. For those of us from the Golden Era if we were still breathing and walking, you could be sure we would turn up to this event and have a wonderful time. However, a few days before the big shindig a select few were invited to a barbecue and that was most enjoyable because we could all let our hair down and wear our "grubbies" if we chose to do so!!! At this particular barbecue I noticed a very sweet-looking man that had a cleric's collar on. I was very curious to who he was. I finally found out and was more than surprised that he was the beautiful little boy that

A day of book signings in May 2007, with Jan & Mickey Rooney.

wrung the tears out of the audience who saw the movie *Boys Town*, with Spencer Tracy and Mickey Rooney. He had a crying scene in it that was just unforgettable and…he was a Watson boy who played Pee Wee in the movie and who was now known as Reverend Bobs Watson!!! We lost dear Bobs in 1999.

Just lately the Watsons and I have added another couple on to our friendship list that also started out very strangely for me, but has added much to my NOW years!

THE NAME IS JONES…D. JONES

The writer Richard Lamparski of the famous books *Whatever Became of…?* was holding a gathering at the Roosevelt Hotel to advertise his newest book and he had invited those of us that he had already written about in previous books as well as his new additions to this gathering. Tony was busy answering questions that a man and his wife wanted to know about vaudeville (no, Tony wasn't in it but he was an expert on that era and had written about it), so I made myself comfortable at the bar and ordered a coke. Sitting beside me was a very quiet gentleman who seemed a bit bored so I thought I'd just break the silence and perhaps make him feel a little bit better.

I don't think it helped much, but I introduced myself and he introduced himself. I hadn't seen him in years and when I mentioned that fact it didn't seem to do anything for him. Not one to give up I kept on talking

With Edith Fellows and Susanna Foster at a private part held by Richard Lamparski.

and things got a little bit better but not so much that it made a heck of a lot of difference. I remembered him and although he recognized my name that was just about the extent of it.

He was sitting alone so I told him if he wanted to he could join Tony and me later on and perhaps we could all get together in the future. He

With Dickie Jones in *Woman Doctor*, 1938.

Together again in 2003.

looked extremely uncomfortable when I asked him to exchange phone numbers with us and although I am not usually a person to push a reluctant acquaintance I couldn't understand his attitude because we had been in a movie together in 1938. He only appeared at the end of the movie but nevertheless he had a marvelous career, then and afterwards. I had also attended one of his birthday parties when we were both very young and still had the press clipping of that so I couldn't understand his attitude. Not one to give up I did call him about a week later and mentioned the movie we had been in and the press clipping that I still had of his birthday party! He had completely forgotten about the 1938 movie, *Woman Doctor*, and you can't blame him because his part was very small as a boy in a wheelchair and let's face it, he must have had tons of birthday parties just like the one I attended. His name was Dickie Jones and apart from the many movies he was in it is an interesting historical fact that he was the voice of *Pinocchio* in the Walt Disney 1940 animated story of that adorable wooden little boy.

After I reminded Dick of our past get-togethers his whole attitude changed and became the warm person that I eventually got to know. It was even better when, at one of the Jivin Jacks and Jills barbecues he introduced me to his dear wife Betty and from then on it was a pleasure to get together with them when he discovered that I wasn't one of "the Hollywood crowd." He disliked that group of people very much because he was now a very down-to-earth business man, a happy husband and father to a big and beautiful family. The incongruity of the whole thing is now that I don't have my darling Tony beside me, my daughter and Phil insisted that I give up my home and come to live with them. I did and Dick and Betty live a stones throw away from us. I am now planning to get the Watsons and the Jones together at our house and that should be fun because we have a lot in common now that we are all older. So you see, there are a lot of good things involved in putting "on a few years." For my young readers, do not despair. There is much to look forward to after the bloom of youth has faded!!! More substance takes place and the things you used to worry about just dissipate into nothing-ness and you discover the wonder of the true priorities that finally becomes the star in your life!

No Expiration Date

I consider myself a very fortunate woman as I look back on my life. I realize that apart for a few potholes that appeared spasmodically on an otherwise pretty smooth personal highway, it's been a full and a good life.

I am now at an age that people often refer to as the age of wisdom and because of that I am asked quite frequently for advice from neophyte actors and actresses (in this era, both referred to as actors) the best way to pursue an acting career and "stay on top of the heap"! I guess my advice is obvious and nothing really cerebral, but it does have its function if carried out.

Unlike most professions where one is selling a product or perhaps "inventing a better mousetrap" one's self worth is not in jeopardy. You are representing an inanimate object.

However, as an actor, your whole persona is up for grabs and, especially at the beginning, when you are at your most vulnerable trying to get a toe hold in a very competitive business. To put it in a very simple term, one has to have the skin of a rhinoceros to succeed as an actor because some experiences are not pleasant ones.

For instance, when you go in for an audition and you are full of expectations and anxious to prove that you have great potential and worthy of being taken seriously, one can melt like hot candle wax when your psyche is pulled apart by those in charge. The incongruity of the situation is that to be a good actor one has to have sensitivity, but that sensitivity can also be one's downfall.

I have seen time after time, cases where actors who have just a shallow talent get ahead because they let derogatory comments or casting couch pitches just roll off their backs and continue to forge ahead. The more sensitive and talented actor very often gets either disillusioned or suffers such a mighty blow to their self confidence that they just give up. Yes, I would say that one of the prime requisites to an acting career is to have a skin of a rhinoceros.

To blow my own horn I think I could have had a wonderful career as a character actress. I know I could have handled the expertise needed for such roles, but I just didn't have the stomach for the necessary moxie it takes to take all of the blows till you have proven yourself. However, that may have been a godsend in my case.

After having returned to this country after spending the years of World War II in South Africa and seeing what all of my contemporaries were going through I made the decision that life was way too short to go through what they were experiencing. They had the facility to become corks.

As soon as they were pushed down, they would pop up and wait out the next dunking. Sometimes it paid off but for the majority it was just heartbreaking that took its toll in many ways: heavy drinking, multiple marriages, deep psychological problems, which led to early graves or sometimes suicide. My timing was just right. Very early on my return to America I met the man I fell deeply in love with and I made him my priority. We would have been married for 58 years but after waging a valiant and courageous fight against lung cancer he passed away in July of 2005. I remember a scene in *All About Eve* where Bette Davis, who is a very famous stage star, and her friend Celeste Holm are stuck in a car in the snow and while waiting for Gary Merrill to come back with some help to get the car going again Bette Davis, who is feeling her age, starts to imagine how lonely life would get if all one could look forward to is to turn over in bed and just see a script there instead of a man who loves you sharing that bed. I think this was the easiest decision I made in my whole life.

I opted for the man and in doing so we produced a beautiful daughter, Toni Maryanna, that gives joy each and every day and remains my husband's and my best legacy.

This may not appeal to everyone but I feel that I've had it all. I loved every single second of my career as a child, I married the man I loved and remained with him for almost 58 years ... Our child has been nothing but an angel to everyone that she comes in contact with and she and her husband added to our lives by giving Tony and me our wonderful grandson Daniel.

I remain on the periphery of show business because I enjoy doing lectures, attending banquets honoring those of us from the Golden Era of Hollywood and I certainly have enjoyed reliving my life through the writing of these two books. I am hoping that the reader has enjoyed the journey. I certainly have.

International Sybil Jason Fan Club

The International Sybil Jason Fan Club is now celebrating its 23rd year and its members are still treated to four publications a year. They include newsletters, magazine articles, personal snapshots from Sybil's own albums, and four 8x10 personally autographed photos of Sybil.

ANNUAL MEMBERSHIP DUES: $12.00 USA
                              $17.00 FOREIGN

MAKE CHECKS PAYABLE TO:
   The International Sybil Jason Fan Club

and SEND TO: Gary L. Heckman
                    745 South 31st. Street
                    Lincoln, Nebraska
                    68510 USA

CHECK THESE TITLES!
BearManorMedia.com
PO Box 71426 • Albany, GA 31708

Spike Jones Off the Record: The Man Who Murdered Music by Jordan R. Young
20th anniversary edition, newly revised & updated!
$29.95   ISBN 1-59393-012-7

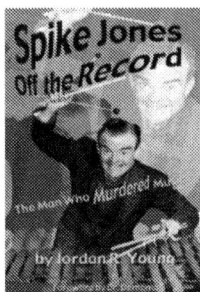

Let's Pretend and the Golden Age of Radio by Arthur Anderson
Revised and expanded, now including a complete log of the show by radio historians Martin Grams, Jr. and Derek Teague!
$19.95   ISBN 1-59393-019-4

It's That Time Again Vol. 2 – More New Stories of Old-Time Radio. Edited by Jim Harmon
New adventures of Red Ryder, Baby Snooks, House of Mystery, The Whistler, Jack Benny and more!
$15.00   ISBN 1-59393-006-2

The Bickersons: A Biography of Radio's Wittiest Program by Ben Ohmart
Lavishly illustrated, with a foreword by Blanche herself, Frances Langford. A complete history of the program. Biographies of the cast. Scripts. The infamous *Honeymooners*/Jackie Gleason court case. Unused material. And much more!
$19.95   ISBN 1-59393-008-9

Private Eyelashes: Radio's Lady Detectives by Jack French
Phyl Coe Mysteries, The Affairs of Ann Scotland, Defense Attorney, The Adventures of the Thin Man, Front Page Farrell...radio was just full of babes that knew how to handle themselves. Get the lowdown on every honey who helped grind a heel into crime.
$18.95   ISBN: 0-9714570-8-5

A Funny Thing Happened On The Way To the Honeymooners...I Had a Life by Jane Kean
Jane Kean tells all—and tells it like it was. Jane Kean, star of Broadway, films and television, has had a career that has spanned 60 years. Jane is perhaps best known as Trixie in the award-winning television series, *The Honeymooners*.
$17.95   ISBN 0-9714570-9-3

For all books and more, visit www.bearmanormedia.com
or write books@benohmart.com. Visa and Mastercard accepted.
Please add $2.50 postage per book. (For Priority mail, please $5.00 postage.)

www.ingramcontent.com/pod-product-compliance
Ingram Content Group UK Ltd.
Pitfield, Milton Keynes, MK11 3LW, UK
UKHW021310180426
11947UKWH00015B/1145